# Cracker Yarns
# Florida Folklore

## Linda Lee

Dedicated to those that came before us, to the
Florida pioneer, to the men and boys that
marched off to war in '61.

I have tried to give life to the rusty tin that peeks from under the
live oaks and hammocks. I have listened to the whispers of the old
homesteads and have gently touched the tombstone of the
unknown.

Our past is quickly being paved over and once gone will be forgot-
ten as fast as the asphalt can dry. I have tried to intertwine their
whispers in a way that allows us to peek into the lives of our brave
and wonderful
Florida pioneers.

# Table of Contents

# A Find In A Weedy Field

I saw the barn between the trees, the weeds had claimed their
space.
I stopped, climbed thru the wire fence and wondered at the place.
The home had long since fallen down, (without a poem or yarn)
Yet here it stood, still fighting on, a simple, cracker barn.
I touched a post half rotten thru, still holding rusted tin,
I let my eyes adjust to shade, then slowly I walked in.
I heard a stomp of heavy foot, from shadows, close, near by,
A tired horse then shook her mane, to rid herself from fly.
Her mane was tangled and unkempt, though back was strong and
wide,
She snatched at grass between the boards, sweat dried upon her
side.
Her harness hung upon a peg, the plow against the wall,
She nickered softly as I left her standing in the stall.
I leaned against a corner board, was warped and had a crack,
I closed my eyes, so I could see and let the years roll back.
I saw the children in the yard, tilling garden row,
Some pulled weeds, some just looked, one leaned against his hoe.
Their feet were bare and skin, tanned brown, I watched as one by
one,
Looked toward the sky to tell the time, there under summer sun.
They hooted, hollered toward the barn, ran by me standing there,
I watched as four kids jumped upon, the back of that ole' mare.
I followed as they rode her out, the children laughed and shrieked
And soon the horse was pulling grass, while they played in the
creek.

*1*

It was not long before the sun, was even with the trees,
The mare slowly plodded home in grass up to her knees.
I watched as house lights all went out, the night grew silent, still.
The frogs and crickets chorused up, but thoughts stayed there until
I felt the creak of rotting board, I stood, lest it should fall
And looked around, there were no kids and no horse in the stall.
I thought what year it could have been, with fields plowed and clear,
When children laughed, rode to the creek and a plow horse stayed in here.
Now here it sits beneath the trees, in fields grown up and dense,
I touch the boards for one last time and crawl thru rusty fence.

*Bell*

## A Florida Volunteer

He pulled the cinch till it was tight,
Then tied his haversack,
Leaned over for his last farewell
And swung upon her back.
He turned just once to take a look,
To burn it in his heart,
For war was raging north of them
And he was now a part
Of Southern men from every state,
To join up in the fray
And soon he'd be there in the midst
Of butternut and gray.
The miles soon were galloped o're,
Past sand hill, hammock, pine,
So quickly men were on the march,
When he signed on the line.
The battles all seemed endless then,
Smoke filtered out the sky,
Gut shot men grew stiff and cold,
As men were piled high.
Horses screamed as bullets whizzed
And cannons belched out smoke,
Some lines moved forward at a run,
While some fell back and broke.
At night the thought of home and love
Would fill his heart and mind,
But morning' light brought battle fronts,
Most up ahead, but some behind.

He felt the ball go in his side,
It knocked him off his feet
And though the rain was pelting down,
All he could feel was heat.
It seemed he could not close his eyes
And coldness in the breeze,
Had fought to take all heat away
And leave him there to freeze.
The men were shot that came to help,
They tried to save despite,
The minie balls, the hungry hogs
That ate so well that night.
She never got a letter home
And years fell all away,
There's now so few to say a prayer
For those that wore the gray.
And no one knows as they walk by,
A widow once lived here
And waved good-by as he rode off,
A Southern volunteer.
And no one knows beneath the earth,
Now buried row by row,
Forgotten soldiers of our past,
Just bones from long ago.
Some houses, graves were never marked,
It's tough to justify,
We hear them now called traitors
As we watch our history die.

## An Old Swing and Memories

The swing I barely once could touch
Hangs lifeless from the tree,
It's rope now frayed and barely there
Reminds me more of me.
It's holding on despite the years
Of time and it's decay,
The home that housed my family here
Has silvered, turned to gray.

*Bell*

The shutters barely hang to life,
The glass lay all in shards
And no one stops to say hello

Or give it their regards.
It's only me that comes around,
Limping on my cane,
Faltering steps into my past
Is all I can reclaim.
I touch a board that's once a swing
And see my momma there,
Taking time to play with me,
Bun tightly holds her hair.
I see my daddy in the field,
His hand upon his brow,
Yet sadly in my mind I know
Their gone and no one now
Will till the fields, close the doors
Or keep my rope swing straight;
Why it's been years since someone's come
Or stood here at the gate.
The trees have taken over,
Home to owl and  hawk.
Along the path I played upon
No one comes to walk.
It's funny how the loneliness
Takes over joy instead,
When memories of childhood
Are but a thin, short thread.
I feel the start of many tears,
Yet once more will pretend,
I walk along the path of time
And youth will never end.
I hold my cane and hobble through
The weeds, the grass and bush.
I close my eyes, remember ck
And give my swing a push.

## A Home's Last Home

It sits back in the thicket
With weeds and trailing vine,
No windows, door to keep out rain,
No help to fight back time.
It waits for one that will not come
To give it yearly trims,
To help regain a little strength
There under mossy limbs.
Foundation rocks have crumbled, slipped
And boards have pulled away,
Where once the nails held them tight,
They've loosened with decay.
For many years it's been forgot,
The family long has died,
And not a soul, at least alive
Has yet to step inside.
Long, hard years have touched this spot
And no one holds the keys
Of who it was that cut the boards
And felled the many trees.
Darkness comes much sooner now
And time will all but fade,
Memories of this cracker house
That rests beneath the shade.
But now it seems someone has come
And fenced the world out
And put up pallet for a gate

With posts, dug deep and stout.
A home that housed a family,
Thru storm and sun and fog
Has fallen now to just a spot
Where someone keeps a dog.
I think it sad that such a place
Tries hard to hold the land,
While people scoff and pass it by,
I'll never understand.
Stare into the eyes of time,
Thru windows with no glass,
Before the weeds and ivy spread
And killed what little grass
Fed the stock the cracker had,
The cow, the goat, the hog
And left the remnants of our past
To house someone's old dog.

*Picture by Ruth Scruggs*

## The Cleanup

I just stopped to get a picture.
The moment that I took
Would not delay my meeting
If I stopped to take a look.
I pushed aside the brambles,
To get closer to the door,
Just to get a better shot,
Was that and nothing more.
But as I neared the vacant house
I saw familiar scar,
Windows broke and boarded up,
The front door was ajar.
The porch could barely hold the rail,
The floor was warped and thin.
I swatted cobwebs in my path
And slowly I walked in.
The heat inside was dusty, dank,
Pulled hair up with a comb
And thru the tangles that fell out,
I looked around the home.
A life was scattered near and far,
Thru out and up the stair,
Tables turned and pictures smashed,
Things piled upon a chair.
Paper strewn about the room,
Glass bird, no tail nor wing,
I wondered who it was that came

And did this dreadful thing.
I slowly looked around the room
And out loud, wondered why ,
When golden hair of collie dog,
Quite sudden, caught my eye.
It was a little worse for wear,
The hair was frizzed and wild,
It must have been a well loved toy,
Once held by little child.
I turned the table right side up,
Stacked old books for a prop,
I held the collie for a time,
Then set him there on top.
I looked at walls that once were new,
Now colors were so faint.
I reached my hand to touch the past
And stroked the peeling paint.
I found a woman's powder box,
It's mirror cracked with fog,
I held it tight till clasp would hold
And put it by the dog.
A few knick-knacks that were not broke,
I saved from off the floor
And put them on the table
As I twice had done before.
I said a prayer for those that passed
And hoped no one would see,
The thoughtless disregard, contempt
Of life, now in debris.
I pulled the door so it would close,
It scraped against the wood.
I saved the treasures that I'd found,
Done all I thought I could.

I walked away with heavy heart,
Old houses had it rough,
It seemed so sad, a hundred years
Would still not be enough,
To show us those that went before
Are ones we should revere
And honor what they left behind.......
The home that was built here.

*Picture by Linda Ball Grohman.*
*I wrote this for her after she told me about her grandmother's home being ransacked. The only things saved were a stuffed dog, a powder box and a few trinkets.*

## The Cup

I had to go to town today, a thing that I despise,
But fridge and cupboards both were bare, I needed some supplies.
I wandered down the grocery aisles, amid the sneeze and cough
And while I heaped my basket full, my mind kept wandering off.
I knew my beds were all unmade, cat hair was on the floor,
I needed to get far away, so I could just ignore
All the things that needed done, while I had gone to town.

I got my paper and my pen and finally I sat down.
I need a little Linda time, a door to enter in,
A place to start my time away, a place I could begin.
I saw this picture late last week, I knew it was a find,

12

It crept into my restless sleep and stayed there on my mind.
Today I think I'll take the walk. This picture was my bait;
I slowly walked the weed choked lane and touched the rusty gate.
The fancy gate was brittle, tied up with leather  strap,
A rusted piece fell to the ground as I pushed to get a gap.
I dug my hands down through the weeds, picked rusty pieces up
And found among the tangled growth, a dainty, flowered cup.
I rubbed off dirt and blew away, the dust and all my smears
And held it gently in my hand and walked back through the years.
The grass had grown round about, the trees, the porch, the floor.
I did not step on rotten boards and made it to the door.
The hall was bare and lonely, the staircase fallen in,
I stopped to let my eyes adjust before I could begin.
The parlor held a bedstead, that was pushed against the wall,
There on the table next to it; a cup, petite and small.
The flowers matched the cup I held, the one found by the gate,
Both finely painted flowery scenes, dainty and ornate.
The curtains long have blown away, the house had lost it's charm.
But then a wisp of yellowed lace brushed against my arm.
She beckoned me to dining room, to table and to chair
And reached for fragile, tiny cup, I held as we sat there.
She told me such sad story, there was no happy part,
She held the cup so close to her, it nearly broke my heart.
She talked of years of waiting, not knowing of his fate,
Of drinking coffee through the day and waiting at the gate.
Her only son had ridden off, to young, was just a prank;
He played the drums and walked the miles, a boy too young for rank.
She told me of her waiting years, not once did she look up,
Her ghostly tears filled haunting eyes and splashed down on the cup.
She moved the chair, held table top and leaned to help her stand,
Then disappeared into the mist, with fragile cup in hand.
I looked around and rubbed my eyes, not grasping what took place,

Was then I saw the shimmered light of old and yellowed lace.
I knew I had a peek thru time, of what went on before,
A mother waiting patiently. A son that went to war.
I stayed a moment, gathered strength, then walked thru weeds and grass,
Stopped a moment by the gate and prayed before I passed.
Atop the weeds and nettles, pushed down by years of weight,
Was tiny, fragile, flowery cup, still waiting at the gate.

## The Fireplace

The embers long have since grown cold,
The brick is worn and cracked,
The plastered walls now grow the mold
And plans it's next attack.
So many years have passed it o're,
Forgotten, now until
I push against an unlocked door
And fight against the chill
Of many years it stood alone
To fight against attack,
Yet proud it stood, unloved, unknown
Until someone came back.
I feel so the pain of grief,
At beauty so decayed,
Yet somehow feel I the thief
Because no one has stayed.
And I like those that went before
Will only look around,
I can not stay to help restore
the treasure that I'd found.
I touch the mantle, wipe the dust,
Stare through the window pane,
I know it's all so sad, unjust
And probably won't remain.
Though wind may blow and floors will creak
Amidst the old, the worn,
Moments from your past will speak

And own a heart that's torn.
I'll walk a bit around the room
And cry at your decay,
Knowing this is but a tomb,
I turn and walk away.

## The Flood

I saw a picture of a house, was just a little shack,
Instead of seeing what was there, my memories flooded back.
Now who can know what sparks the mind and sends it on a roll,
Remembering buried times of life that we lived long ago?
I try to keep my memories, clear and neatly filed,
But this old house led me back to days I was a child.
I studied boards that held it up, could barely just survive
And thru the dusty years of time, transported me to five.
The years of youth are quickly spent, we barely are aware,
Of slower walk, weakened eyes, of gray and thinning hair.
So often times I take a walk and fight against the fog,
Till I am just a five year old and have my collie dog.
We once again walk the trails of youth, both she and I.
But I grew up and she grew old, still walking by my side.
I watched my father on that day, the day I saw him weep,
That awful day that cancer choose, to have her put to sleep.
I keep her picture by my desk, her collar in my drawer,
So many dogs I've had since then, but none I have loved more.
A furry horse a neighbor bought and told me he was mine,
He often bucked, taught me to ride, when I had just turned nine.
The magic of a child and horse, is freedom in your hand,
For those who never held the rein will never understand.
I snipped a piece of his old tail, I still have to this day
And cried into his graying mane, the day we moved away.
The years passed very quickly, had a husband and a child,
When he informed me he had bought a stud colt, young and wild.
A horse that he had never seen, was never touched before,

17

Just told me he was stocking
red, would never tell me more.
At first sight I said, "Let's go
home, he's wild as a coot."
I prayed he'd break his skinny
neck while he was in the chute.
But husband just proceeded on,
colt now frothy foam,
Roped and tied his very first
and he was coming home.
I watched as he began to grow,
fill body out and mind,
The boney colt had grown up
and wild had turned to kind.
We must have rode a million
miles, on and off the grids,
He aged with me, but then went on to raise all of our kids.
Thirty-four had slowed him down, the horse I loved, adored,
Would now lay down the final time and rise for me no more.
Again I snipped a strand of tail, still red with wisps of gray,
It's in a drawer with other things I've saved onto this day.
And now it's time for me to think of something that I dread,
I can not touch the scissors, though I know what lies ahead.
He lays there sleeping on my lap, for more than twenty years.
I hear him purr, I watch him fail and curse the day that nears.
Soon another memory of life that went before
Will be beside two strands of tail and collar in my drawer.
A picture of an old home place, just a little shack,
Instead of seeing what was there, my memories flooded back.

# The House

I heard them long before I saw, the tramping of a thousand feet.
It did not matter, on they came, thru winter's cold and summer's
heat.
They bivoacked near the garden gate, burned fence board for their
fire,
Dug up the graves in yonder field, left nothing but the briar.
They hooted late into the night, curses filled each room,
The cotton crop, the daffodils all refused to bloom.
And so it went that each new camp would leave with more and
more,
So soon the mistress had to flee the lingering yankee war.
They tore up floor boards, smashed my glass, slashed curtains for
their fun,
Searched for treasure in my floor, shot stock so we had none.
They fowled wells with swollen pets, torched everything but me,
Twice I saw our soldiers come and twice the yanks did flee.
They brought their bleeding to my halls, filled every room and bed.
Soon all my carpets held the stain of all the yankee dead.
Bullet holes now pock my walls and birds fly up the stair,
Piano parts are strewn about, midst scattered books and chair.
I strain to hear my mistress' voice, the master's hearty laughs,
But all that filters into me is dust between the shafts.
And so the years have rolled on by, my pillars bravely try,
To keep the walls from spilling in, but more and more the sky
Is taking over marbled tile and neglectful years have cast,
The silence of a gloomy death, I know I can not last.
I strain to hear the childish voice, to see the fields of white,

But days of glory have now passed, I welcome in the night.
But yesterday a woman came and touched my crumbling wall,
I saw her shudder just a bit, then walk down center hall.
She stood and gazed through broken glass, I saw her shed a tear,
So long it's been, a touch of life, since someone entered here.
She stroked the door on it's last hinge, she climbed the crumbling stair.
I strained to hear the creak of wood, for years no one stepped there.
She bent and picked up old bed spring and polished off the rust;
For only wind has moved around and swept away the dust.
I saw her touch the penciled marks of names and written prose,
All left behind by conquerors, by Yankees I suppose.
I watched for hours as she walked, then sitting in the light
Of broken window she began  to tremble and to write.
I know she saw what I had seen, the beauty, now decay,
I knew she saw the marching men, the blue clad and the gray.
She tarried here for quite some time, through house and untilled ground,
I watched her slowly walk away, she stopped then turned around.
So still she stood for quite a time, till evening sun grew black.
I whispered, "Pillars please hold on, this one is coming back."

## The Lamb of God

Mary had a little lamb
Two thousand years ago.
He left the throne of heaven
For a manger here below.
Born to be the sacrifice
As bulls and lambs before,
Their blood would only cover sins,
Spilled ore' and ore' and ore'.
Mary birthed the lamb of God,
His blood would cleanse our sin,
No sacrifice from bulls and goats
Could cleanse without, within.
This was the child that was to come,
For prophesy foretold;
A Savior born in Bethlehem
Wrapped in the swaddling fold.
Mary had a little lamb
And tidings were all glad.
The shepherds bowed and knew he was
The best that heaven had.
God looked down upon his son,
I'm sure he felt the loss,
As Jesus slept in Mary's arms
God saw the future cross.
Mary had a little lamb,
Tempted, without sin,
From manger to the wooden beam,

Would feel the nails go in.
He'd feel the weight of sacrifice,
The hammer's heavy slam,
Began that night in Bethlehem
When Mary had the lamb.

*Fort White*

## The Long Road Home

Dusty puffs of roadbed settled back where he had stepped,
While dampened grass from mornin' dew, marked where the man
had slept.
He had a shirt, threadbare and thin, that crumbled at the touch,
His pants were patched and dirty brown, he leaned upon a crutch.
A tree limb from a jagged fork, whittled to his size,
Helped him hobble down the road, with a free hand to shade eyes.
The lonely path that led to home, was dusty, hot and long;
But slow the miles passed away, for weak men and the strong.
Beside the ditch lay bones exposed, of someone on his way,
Some tattered cloth, a bit of wool, in shades of southern gray.
So slow he knelt and pulled the dirt, to cover scattered bones,
Wiped his brow, stood on his crutch, pressed closer unto home.
The blackened hulks of chimneys stood in contrast to the green
Of weedy fields now springing up, that grew there in between
The fences without board nor post, wells fouled with decay,
The soldier sadly shook his head and hobbled on his way.
He came upon a cool creek and pushed aside debris;
Soaked his festering, swollen wound, in shade of splintered tree.
His body ached, he closed his eyes,  he lay there on the ground
And noticed not the other men that came and gathered round.
Each soldier standing straight, now healed, a regiment in gray,
They left his crutch by splashing creek, walked Southward on their way.
Now the coolness of that spot has often brushed my cheek,
I lean against a gnarled tree and stare into the creek.

## The Muse

If eyes are windows to the soul,
I saw a glimpse of long ago,
Thru curtains that were tattered, torn,
Protecting frail, old, forlorn,
From things, perhaps, we're not to know.

I pondered there, so still I stood
And wondered if I even should,
Turn my back and walk away
And leave this place of such decay,
But no, I reached out, touched the wood.

In just an instant I could see
And hear the spirit calling me,
I listened to a wispy wail,
It came from someone old and frail,
A wrinkled hand held out the key.

I knew that no one could exist,
But mind was trying to insist
That this was something that was real,
More than spirits I could feel,
A strangeness in the rising mist.

He beckoned me to come inside.
He straightened up, as if his pride
Would make his stories seem more true,
Was just a moment, maybe two...
The morning now was eventide.

His shaky hand turned up the lamp,
He told me of a soldier's camp
In a time so long ago,
He talked of heat, of driving snow,
Of sleeping in the cold and damp.

His voice then softened just a bit,
There on the wall just opposite,
A picture with a man and gun,
His uniform from World War l,
The old man stopped, I thought he quit.

He mumbled grandson, wiped a tear,
I knew then he would preserve,
But did not know how long he'd last,
Reliving stories of his past
And mixing them from year to year.

Amid the papers, all askew,
He tightly held to just a few,
Then something seemed to catch his breath,
He showed me clipping s of a death,
Of great grandson he never knew.

It seemed he also went to war,
Signed up to be in army corps,
His medals shone like silver chrome,
But this young man did not come home,
The old man stopped and said no more.

For several minutes he stood there,
He seemed perplexed and unaware
In darkened shadows of the room,
In dismal house that was his tomb.
I wondered at this whole affair.

Then slowly he began to speak,
He smiled some and touched my cheek.
"I saw you stop as you walked by,
I saw you look, I heard you sigh,"
He said to me in voice so weak.

"I knew someone would feel me near,
Would stop a moment, have no fear.
It seemed so long, but not to soon,
You touched the logs that I had hewn,
Did more than take a picture here."

The lantern gave up all it's light,
It was high noon, was no more night.
The man, the stories faded way,
With two great wars and one in gray,
I hurried home, began to write.

*Fort White*

# The Old Man and the Bridge

I stare at pictures from the past
And feel privileged,
To see the life of Mr. Will,
Atop the wooden bridge.
There's oyster shells upon the road,
A Plymouth just behind,
I stare at all the piney woods,
Till stories fill my mind.
The photograph has faded date,
Was nineteen-thirty two,
When oyster shells were our main roads
And Florida was new.
They called him Will, the cracker man,
Of pine woods in his day,
He leaned upon his gun and cane
And took the time to pray.
Though he is gone, his picture stays,
His memory will remain;
The grand dad looking o'er the bridge
And leaning on his cane.
I wonder at his memories?
What gave him tears or joy,
When Florida was pine hill, swamp
And he was but a boy.
Times were rough when roads were dirt,
But turtles, deer and hog,
Were heaped beside the greens and squash,

The possum an the frog.
I wonder as he stands atop,
The river, high and dry,
If in the waters rushing past
Are memories floating by.
I see the dusty roadbeds
And I search them for a clue,
When Grand dad was a young man
And Florida was new.
I see him building General Store,
Though hindered in his stride,
The Kellum's Store was grand dad's place,
The best in Riverside.
His store receipts might take a month,
Before the bills were paid,
While others, more down on their luck,
Would try to make a trade.
He saw the forests thinning out,
Saw buildings start to rise,
Saw the bridges being built,
The land, more civilized.
And often on a summer's eve,
He'd light a pine knot torch,
And gaze out on the land he knew
While rocking on the porch.
And while he rocked there was a hand,
That he had loved to hold,
And both the Kellum's saw life change,
While both were growing old.
Now there he stands atop the bridge,
Not one cane now but two,
And ponders back upon the years,
When Florida was new.

*James William Kellum, grandfather to Linda Bennie McNeil Thomas, taken at Duck Pond Marina, San Juan Ave. Jacksonville*

# The Pasture Shack

It was just a wee and little shack,
Not built by any code.
It sat beneath the pasture trees
And way back from the road.

So many times I walked the path
That led me to the yard.
I picked my way thru limb and brush,
Sidestepped the window shards.

On many walks I took grandkids,
To let them look around;
We'd find a shell, a rusty pot
That lay upon the ground.

The buckets, boards told stories,
Some short and some were long;
We'd touch the boards along the wall,
Some rotten, some still strong.

We sat upon the rusty springs
That once held those asleep.
They'd look around for little things,
Some treasure they could keep.

Each time they came I studied them,
Hoped stories that we told,
Would stay with them as they have me
Now that I'm growing old.

I prayed that as the years all passed,
Those moments would not die
And all the tried and olden things
Be seen thru Mamaw's eyes.

For now the shack no longer stands,
A place time has forgot,
But I remember walking here
Telling stories on this spot.

I pray in years when they are old
They do what I once done....
Tell stories in a run down shack
To daughter and to son.

I pray they always see much more
Than rusty bed or chair.
I hope they squint their eyes and see
What they saw when I was there.

*Gulf Hammock*

# The Perfume Bottle

I walked into the dusty room, amid the trash, the dirt and gloom;
And there it was against the wall, unkempt and broken, three feet
tall.
I smelled the softness of perfume.
Her brush lay on the bureau there, with strands of gold and
reddish hair,
With drawers ajar and half pulled out, there were no signs of her
about,
Yet perfume wafted in the air.
A pair of shoes upon the floor and traces of the years before
Were mingled there without a clue, yet all looked like a rendezvous
With perfume one could not ignore.
There on the bed, unmade, unkempt, where years before someone
had slept,
I saw a note with flowing script and spots where age old ink had
dripped
Upon the floors that no one swept.
The paper, faded, thin and frayed, in pieces now, almost decayed
Were words from someone long ago and so the words began to
flow
In this house of disarray.
I looked around, was no one there, yet perfume filled the musty
air.
I gently lifted, blew the dust and waited for eyes to adjust
Before I read of sad affair.
It seems her children all have left, there's not much here for one to
cleft,

They left when young and now she's old, they told her then, "Must get it sold."
And now it shows the years of theft.
Her letter said she could not bare to sell the house in disrepair,
To think of those she loved and raised, how they all left, ignored, unphased,
Yet still her perfume fills the air.
She said the robbers came at night, she was to old to hide, take flight,
That she was lucky to survive, to write this down, to be alive,
She was to old to shoot or fight.
Her letter told of how she shook, just to afraid to take a look,
She wasn't sure, one thief or two, she 116just prayed, stayed out of view118
And cried at all the robbers took.
She told me where to go, exhume, to look no further than this room,
She did not say just what she did and did not tell me what she hid,

Was then I found her old perfume.
There amid a pile of trash, windows broke and curtains slashed;
A bottle signed with "I love you," with not a bit of residue,
I found the bottle, top half smashed.
It lay atop a little card, signed with 'Love and our regard,
You know we'd like to visit you, but Meg has children, I have two
And getting there would be to hard."
In disarray I found each room, a day in time, a gloomy tomb.
I knew each child had taken part in breaking pieces of her heart
And yet she held to their perfume.
To enter into other spheres, to feel their hurt, to face their fear,
It takes a toll on sleepy thought, when in between you now are caught
And captive of the words you hear.

# The Room

Like junk forgotten in a bin,
Not thought of there in years,
dust settled on my hair and skin,
I took a breath and entered in
And waited there for dust to clear.

Aged floor joists, roughly hewn,
Where planks have rotted way,
I plunked a key, was not in tune,
I carefully walked among the ruin
And looked about the sad array.
A memory snuck from up behind,
familiar, long ago,
A place forgotten, yet I find,
It plays there often in my mind,
Of things not seen, but yet I know.

I know I've walked here many times,
When sleep escapes my grip.
I watch the ivy slowly climb,
Things covered slow by dirt and grime,
Decaying more with each new trip.

I close my eyes and once again,
See memories I have filed,
Of misty homes, forgotten kin,
Wispy memories from within,
From days I was a little child.

I hear my grandma playing there,
The memory like a torch,
That burns the faint and burns the fair,
While we grow old so unaware,
Of those that sat upon this porch.

In sleepless nights I visit here
And walk where there is dirt and mold,
What is forgotten, I revere
And cling to memories I hold dear,
Important now as I grow old.

I pray my grandkids are not conned,
But see the worth in dust and gloom.
I hope they always will respond,
See past the old and far beyond,
And take a step into the room.

## The Shuttered Window

Birds flitter in the treetops
Above the cracked bird bath,
And bricks lay strewn along the side
Of winding garden path.
Moss has grown beneath the shade,
The winding path now slick,
There's none that walk beneath the trees
Or step upon the brick.
For Spanish Moss has taken o're,
It surely left it's mark,
Sways in the breeze of morning sun
And storms that come at dark.
No longer do I gaze upon
A scene of sweet repose,
No fragrance wafts up to my panes
Of lily's and of rose.
And as the gardens fall away
My shutters start to hang
And midst the hoot owl's noisy screech,
My shutters start to bang.
The winds have pushed upon my glass,
The rain has sent it's spray;
The roaches, mice and coon have come,
Since all have moved away.
No one has wiped the years of dirt
That I've tried to withstand;
There's smudges of a child's nose

And prints of little hand.
A cradle sits beneath my sill,
It's rocking long has stopped,
A blanket, thread bare by the door,
Not moved since it was dropped.
There's always hope before I break
And splinter into shards,
Someone will find the winding path
That leads them to the yard.

*Old home in Bell*

They'll fill the birdbath, cut the weeds,
Put bricks back in their place,
Wipe my panes with thirsty cloth
And cover me with lace.
They'll oil the wooden cradle here
And tidy up the room
And let me look out on the path
That winds through moss and bloom.

Forgotten years are gaining now,
So slow they seem to pass.
I fight against the sun and storm,
They fight against my glass.
For time has stolen history
And claimed what it can take,
I fought it all and stayed intact,
But ready now to break.
When shards of me will litter ground,
Just I will feel the loss,
And weathered pieces of my past
Will mingle with the moss.

# The Sign

They say it's there to keep you, from falling thru the floor,
'No Trespassing' is taped upon the window in the door.
It's there to keep you from within, keep secrets all inside,
Darkness in the ransacked rooms is all that can reside.
But whispers sneak thru broken glass, where owls, ravens fly,
Tis just the humans who can read, while only some comply.

'No Trespass' sign was plain in view, was there for all to see.
I looked around and told myself, "It wasn't meant for me."
The double parlor just inside, in plain view of my sight,
I pushed against the rotted door, but dead bolt held it tight.

I stepped into a window, it's shards lay all about,
The floors were covered in the glass, with silence in and out.
The dusty rooms were dark and dank, I touched a crumbling wall,
Holding to the stair rail, that quivered, lest it fall.
Medallions on the ceiling were cracked in disrepair,
Two baby coons turned to look, then scampered up the stair.
The mantle on the fireplace was stained with all the smoke,
While pieces of a giant clock would never sound a stroke.
I watched my step upon the stairs, walked down the center hall,
Marveled at the paper still attached to bedroom wall.
The old floor creaked, was rotted thru places in the room,
Two iron beds, side by side, with plaster as their tomb.
I stood awhile and let my mind take in this house so sad
And put together stories of the life that it once had.
I take an oath there to myself, to quietly ignore
And follow critters past the sign that's hanging from the door.

# The Smoker

I sit and ponder picture,
Till I hear the floor boards squeak,
Stare at shadows from the past
And wait for one to speak.
The whispers pull me back in time,
Their waiting just inside,
One steps forth with outstretched hand
To be my chosen guide.
The screen door squeaks in protest,
The room is dark and bare,
I notice boards are missing
From the old and worn stair.
Most windows have been boarded,
Though tiny shafts of light
Send dusty trails of outside sun
Thru  rooms, as if for spite.
I can see no one before me,
My eyes adjust and scan,
Amid the scurry of the mice,
The presence of a man.
Thru foggy mist of many years,
I know I am allowed,
To see the man that beckoned me,
His shoulders bent and bowed.
His outstretched hand is calloused,
His arms are wrinkled, thin,
Hair as coarse as cotton

Matched the whiskers on his chin.
We both stood there in silence,
He rolled a skinny smoke
And took the longest draw I've seen,
Exhaled and then he spoke.
"I watched as you were walking
And when you were quite near,
I knew that you were different
And knew that you would hear,
All the whispers that came forth,
The loud, the soft, the small,
All the words held captive
In these rooms and down the hall."
He studied me, then dropped his smoke
And squashed it with his heel,
"I knew you'd come to look within
And did not come to steal."
I felt the others all around,
But could not see a face,
The burdens of a hundred years
Have taken o're this place.
The white washed walls have all turned gray
And I could feel the gloom,
The empty years of negligence
Has filled up every room.
He rolled another cigarette,
Said, "This is all that's left,
Locked doors don't stop crooked men,
Their thievery or theft.
Within these walls, a hundred years
Of livin' has been had,
But peeling' paint an unconcern
Now seems to bring the bad.
I've grown weary of my plight,

I can not keep them out,
You will be the last of those
That ever walk about.
For soon they come to take it down,
To pull at boards an floor
And dirt will be my legacy,
A bare spot, nothing more."
A breeze had found it's way inside,
The lingering smoke had cleared,
This photo was in front of me,
The old man disappeared.
Had I walked into this house?
It's long been taken down.
But as I stare at old porch rails,
I feel him standing 'round.
I write these lines and feel him near....
Remember what he spoke,
Now house is gone and he has left,
But I still smell the smoke.

*Picture by Bob Shuker*

44

## The Spirits

Who can know a Southron's heart,
What makes it beat so fast,
While standing on the sacred ground
That honors Southron past.
Who can know the depths of pride,
To stand upon the ground
And wonder at the ghosts that watch,
The spirits gathered 'round.
The wind lay still as I stood there,
So few they'd been that come,
So few would stop to hear the guns,
The bugle, fife and drum.
I stood awhile, lost in my thoughts,
Rocked there to and fro,
Unaware that they were there..
The past of long ago.
I did not know they watched for me,
Were waiting till I came,
I did not see the line of gray
Next to the soldier's name.
I offered up a quick salute,
Left Southron flag in place
And did not notice breeze begin,
That blew around my face.
I turned but once and saw the flag,
Waving there that night,
Unaware of men in gray

That watched, just out of sight.
Soon I'll know the Southron wind
That touched my face and hair,
Were all the men that went before,
The ones I thought not there.
For though I came and stood alone
By monument and plaque,
The wind were whispers of the men
That all saluted back.

*My front yard.*

## The Trip

I've a wedding to prepare for, with so much left to do;
A hurricane that threatens, the wedding 'fore it's through,
An election that's gone crazy, with lies, half truths and crap;
I can't get any sleep at night, to angry for a nap.
I've prayed a lot for patience, but about to lose my grip,
So thought I better take the time and plan a little trip.
I wandered down a wooded path, found stairs for me to climb,
And there before my frazzled eyes, a place lost back in time.

*Fort White*

I pushed quite easy on the door, the wood was old and thin,
I moved aside the porch debris and slowly I walked in.
The curtains were in tatters, the home had seen abuse,
The walls had peeling paper from a hundred years of use.

I touched the worn piano keys, heard every sour note,
I took out paper and my pen and this is what I wrote.
"It's funny how a ragged chair, not fit for a behind,
Could hold you like a lover's arms and clear a troubled mind."
I sit and study every inch from light shafts thru the door,
I see the trail of rats and mice, to carpet on the floor.
I see the cross upon the top of keyboards, worn and old,
I smell the years of emptiness, the dust, the dirt, the mold.
The filtered light shines through the room, time seems to be no
threat,
I softly blow away the dust, hope springs eternal yet.
I spend an hour, maybe two and feel a wee bit stronger,
I move the chair to face the door and sit awhile longer.
I hold the peace that distance gives, but dare not cross the line,
I say good bye to years ago and step back into mine.

# The Trunk

I walked into the auction house, my husband gave a sigh,
Just thought I'd look around a bit, not knowing what to buy.
They had a bit of this and that, some gems, but mostly junk,
Until I walked way in the back and saw a ragged trunk.
Two hours passed, they called the lot, was nearly nine o'clock,
They pulled the worst of all the trunks, onto the auction block.
My husband tried to hold my hand, they tried to lift the lid,
"A mystery, tis locked,", they said, I got the highest bid.
He grumbled as we got it home, he thought it full of lead,
He gave me tools to break the lock, then he went on to bed.
I touched the rusty, worn latch, as gently as I could
And ran my fingers down the side, of dry and splintered wood.
Somewhere between the truck and house, the things the trunk had hid,
Became unlocked and I could now lift the heavy lid.
The musty smell of years gone by wafted in the air.
I stopped a moment, then I touched a lock of golden hair.
A faded ribbon bound the strands, as fragile as a tear,
A fleeting smell of perfume passed, to let me know she's near,
I pressed the golden strands to cheek, it tingled on my skin,
I said a prayer for what I'd find before I looked within.
Twas  yellowed, lacy collar, with a note in flowing script,
"This collar was about my neck, the day my locks were snipped."
A tin type of a tall, young man, holds rifle in his hand
And in the case it also held, a snip of golden strand.
A Bible, pages old and worn, the paper, fragile, thin,
The names of all those gone before, so carefully written in.
I touched the names of long ago, of husband and of wife,

And know within the written page are things held dear in life.
I carefully close the cover and parts of bridal wreath,
My hands begin to quiver as I see what lays beneath.
Was there between the layers, of paper all pressed down,
A locket with two pictures in the folds of wedding gown.
Gingerly I take it out and lay it to the side,
The golden lock, the silken veil, the memories of a bride.
I smell the perfume once again, I wonder could it be,
Could she have left allotted spot, be sitting next to me?
I hesitate and look around, stare at the golden locks,
Then there within the trunk I see, a tiny music box.
I stroke the carved out cover, but leave it where it lays,
The perfume is now stronger and the box begins to play,
A haunting tune of long ago, my mind tells me it's false,
But there it plays as if today, it's played it's first slow waltz.
I see a button, see a thread and think at first it's mud,
A frockcoat folded underneath, the arm was stained in blood.
The music box is playing still, I fear my heart will break,
When there beneath the old frock coat was  framed, beloved keepsake.
An oval picture, clouded glass, in shades of gray and brown,
An aged man in uniform, his aged wife in gown.
And there beneath the picture, was the clipping, James Lee Hyde,
The day of birth, his war time deeds, the year and  day he died.
The music box has slowed it's waltz, a century to the day,
A hundred years have passed and now her perfume fades away.
I gently put things in the trunk, picture, gown and  frock.
A moment after lid is down, I hear the click of lock.
Years pass, it's in the corner, under watchful eye,
The lock has never opened, I check as I walk by.
My husband says I'm crazy, but I wear his words with pride,
He's never heard the music box, smelled  perfume, looked inside.
Is she waiting for a hundred years, when someone sees the junk,
And raises  hand to get in  bid, and buys the ragged trunk?

# The Wayward Trail

He leaned against the withered tree
Until his mind was still,
His shattered leg had felt the heat,
His body felt the chill.
The sweat had long since burned his eyes,
While flies encrust his mouth,
He lifted tree limb for a cane
And slowly he walked south.
Past unkempt fields and smoldering homes,
Past chimneys in the lane,
A swollen mule about to burst,
A horse, just tail and mane.
He shuffled slowly in the sun
On roads just now a trail;
This Southron soldier walking home,
Gunshot and weak and frail.
He brushes flies from off his wound,
His breath just barely comes,
He wonders if the rumbling near
Is thunder or is drums.
His eyes see no horizon,
His walk now slows to stop,
He holds the crooked cane branch,
Stands shaking, lest it drop.
A mother's child can do no more
And slowly slips away,
Blood has seeped and puddled close

To tattered bits of gray.
The years have passed this lonely spot
And no one has come near;
No one has ever come upon
this Southron volunteer.
The winds have swept the tattered cloth
While bears have chewed the bone,
And nothing marks the wayward trail
That never led to home.

## Through The Whispers of Time

I always wonder who it is
That lies beneath the sod,
Stone inscribed, birth, name and death,
While others known to God.
I touch the coldness of the stone,
Each marker, neat and trim
And stand awhile in the shade
Of mossy covered limb.
I close my eyes and blot it out,
The sadness of the view
And soon amid death's quietness,
The living filter through.
I see the columns, weary, tired,
Some shoeless marching forth
And in the distance I can see
The columns of the north.
So soon the smoke has filled the trees,
There's bullets whizzing by,
Some kneel and first line fires off,
Some live and some will die.
The din of battle shakes my heart,
I see one soldier fall,
The cannon shakes the ground when fired,
'tween thuds of minie ball.
A horse has bolted, now it fell,
It stands with just a bruise,
I watch spellbound at what I see,

While rider never moves.
I blink, for I just can not bear
The scene that lays before,
Once gallant men, so full of life,
When first they went to war.
I wipe the sweat from off my brow,
The fighting seemed so near,
I once again see all the graves,
It is so quiet here.
I'd like to think their all aware
Of those who gather 'round,
Their people come in reverence
And love this scared ground.
I touch the bark of gnarled tree,
Feel tears that burn my eye,
I now can scan vast mounds of men,
Then softly say good-by.

## Time Claims the Discarded

I stand and ponder what I see
And strain for words I want to hear,
This cracker home beneath the tree
Was shelter for a pioneer.

The windows are all boarded shut
Briars have now taken o're,
The yard is weeds and needs a cut,
I stare to see what was before.

What others look as aged blight,
Ready for bulldozer's shove,
I see walls all painted white
And know one time it had been loved.

I walk the yard and let the mist
Help me see and understand,
Thru the years how it exists,
Until I see a calloused hand.

The hand that held the walking plow,
Caught the fish and cleaned the deer,
I hoped they could not see it now,
This crumbling home of pioneer,.

A woman who birthed daughter, son,
Grew the garden, shelled the peas,

Did the work till it was done
And shivered in the winter freeze.

The stovepipe still juts from the wall,
I wondered if for food or heat........
Though cracker home begins to fall,
It fights thru time and fights defeat.

Will those that follow thru the years
Push against a centuries theft
And think again of pioneers
When not one cracker home is left?

*Bell*

## Two Thousand and Nineteen

We leased it out in forty-three
When I was just a kid,
With all the boxes piled high
I ran away and hid.
Momma said we would be back
When better days came 'round,
When corn and cotton grew again
And water wet the ground.
Daddy sat out on the porch,
His fields in disarray,
Grandma leaned against the rail
And watched dirt blow away.
I looked back once as mule clopped,
I tried but could not speak,
Daddy slapped the mule's back
And crossed the dried up creek.
A man in shiny truck had stopped,
Clothes pressed and shoes all shined,
He touched his hat and nodded,
Then pointed to the sign.
I could not bear to turn around,
But knew he took it down,
Was way back then in forty-three
We all moved into town.
And so the years have all passed on,
I've more than I had planned
And beg my son to take me back

While I can yet still stand.
He stopped the truck out on the road,
I tried hard to explain,
"Let me go first and look around,"
I leaned  upon my cane.
Boarded windows told no tales,
Of humans, not a trace,
Grazing cows had kept the grass
From covering up the place.
Ivy blotted out sunlight
That filtered in my room.
The porch where last my Daddy sat
Was dank and dark with gloom.
My cane began to wobble then,
I reached out for the door,
The hinges barely held it there,
From falling to the floor.
Soon my son was calling me
To ask how long I'd be.
I waved him off and hobbled back
To June of forty-three.
Birds began to chirp again
And shadows slow revealed,
Cotton, corn were all waist high
And grew in every field.
Roses that my grandma grew
Wound 'round the trellis gate
And Daddy gripped, it would not close
From stems and thorns and weight.
I slowly sat down on a stair
Where one by one I'd climb,
Said yes to all the memories
That called me back in time.
I saw my Momma shelling peas

Close by the kitchen door
And told myself this was the place
That I would leave no more.
I bowed my head and sat awhile,
Then swallowed silent cries,
The shiny truck just right outside
Helped me to close my eyes.
I guess my son has finally come,
I hear his footsteps near,
My spirit wafts up thru the rooms,
I am no longer here.
The creek runs full and now I play,
No fear from jump or fall,
The rain has come and blessed the fields,
The corn and cotton tall.
For now I rest my weary soul,
I need no cane to lean,
My home has called me back again...
Two thousand and nineteen.

*Bell*

# The View From The Road

The trees and ivy do their part,
Tell tendrils to grow fast,
The branches twine with weeds and vine
To cover up the past.
When man now ceases to control,
Push back thru nature's wall,
Neglect the freeze, the summer breeze,
The growth of spring and fall,
It's then the timbers lose their grip
And slowly start to rot,
The wind and rain, sun, hurricane
Will take what man forgot.
Then slowly it begins to fall,
With no more strength to fight,
The roof gives way to dark and day
And creaks there in the night.
The armadillo, mice and owl
Will fight to stay within
And very soon, the snake and coon
Will watch the spider spin.
The termites swarm and circle here,
Tis now a funeral wreath,
Though overgrown, it's now their home,
They fight to live beneath.
The hay has long since blown away,
The harness taken down,
The bird, the bat, the wild cat,

The roof now rusty brown
Still hold to rafters hewn from trees
Grown by master hand,
Without a flinch, things grow by inch
And strangle with each strand.
The trees will soon have shaded o're
And nature will prepare,
No more litter, home to critter,
And no one knows it's there.
What once stood proud in fields all tilled
Have weeds about to choke,
While poison sumac, trees and bees
Grow in the poison oak.
It won't be long before it's gone
And man will never know,
The dry, the wet and all the sweat
From years so long ago.
I stand and stare and look upon
That old and rusty tin.
I try to squint and get a hint
Of what remains within.

*Atop a hill in Gilchrist County*

# Of Walks and Quilts

It was a day in Spring of sixty-three,
I saw her sitting there beneath the shade,
She was sobbing, disheveled and unmade
Yet holding to a quilt upon her knee.
I'd taken Mother to a family grave
When we first saw the woman sitting there.
Her hand was holding back her auburn hair.
She looked but she did not return our wave.
She seemed so sad and mourning there alone,
I almost felt like going to her side,
But she was old and I was young, unknown
So thought it best to smile and keep my pride.
Before we left she knelt to touch a stone.
It was then her sobbing stopped and how she cried.

It was then her sobbing stopped and how she cried,
It chilled me to the bottom of my soul,
Mother touched my hand and waited for control.
We wondered who it was that had just died.
Still now I see the woman in my dreams.
I hear the sobs that wrench and break a heart
And in my troubled sleep she plays a part,
Her sobbing touched my soul, so now it seems.
I kneel beside my coverlet and pray,
Each morning as I rise from rumpled bed.
I do not know the words I am to say
So I weep for the woman there instead.

I got a note from Mother yesterday,
It seems the graveyard woman's fame has spread.

It seems the graveyard woman's fame has spread,
The grandson that she lost was also known
And the quilt that she sits and sews has grown
While she spends her hours grieving for her dead.
I went to visit Mother just last week.
We walked amid the marble of the tombs,
The shaded path beneath the dogwood blooms.
We saw her there but still she did not speak.
The sewing by her side was neatly piled.
She touched it while her one hand held the cane.
I marveled at the love for this dear child,
Unmindful of the sun, the snow, the rain.
Within my soul my heart beat slow then wild,
The woman's sobs rushed over me again.

The woman's sobs rushed over me again,
As lonely as the night before the dawn.
In that moment her final breath was drawn,
A smile replaced her look of grief and pain.
Together now they lay beneath the fern,
Her casket lining is the quilt she made.
His life was sewn together 'neath the shade
While patiently she waited for her turn.
Now on a certain day when weather clears,
I visit Mother for a cup of tea.
We speak of things that happened through the years,
Sometimes we speak of tombstones and a tree
And often while we talk I feel the tears,
It was a day in Spring of eighty-three.

*Quilt Museum in Trenton*

# When Time Has Come

The winds of time have taken toll, no laughter nor a cry;
Dead memories from so long ago, just shadows passing by.
No wagon ruts from off the road, no scythe to cut the grass,
The old beams carry heavy load and watch for one to pass.
The breezes play among the rooms, the walls just hold their
breath.
The heavy air again resumes and nightly calls out death.
The breeze, the wind, the constant hum will stay here sure as not.
Each house will look for one to come before the beams all rot.
Their spirit twines amongst the dust and holds to what it can,
To see it now, it's so unjust, just dying without plan.
And soon the time will come to pass when beauty is no more;
An indentation on the grass of what stood years before.

*Bell*

65

# When a Place Talks

McCulley's Farm, Jasper, Fl.

I saw her there the day she stopped,
Close to my rusty roof.
She slid from off her horse's back
And checked the mare's hoof.
And for a moment it was if,
I turned into my prime,
A horse was standing right out front
And turned back hands of time.
Yep, someone stopped out front today,
My past came rushing back,
To a time when roof was new,
Before I was a shack.
When men would gather at my door,
Spend time to talk or swap,
'bout weather, horses, who had died,
'bout rain and 'bout a crop.
How often then when I was young,
I'd hear the horses lope,
When harness would be hung on pegs,
Both saddles, bridles, rope.
The smithy used to be 'round back,
His forge there in the shade,
But years have passed since he or I
Have heard a horse that neighed.
The  years have been so silent,

My roof's 'most rusted through;
Yet just today someone has stopped
To check a loosened shoe.
My boards have splintered, rotted some,
My roof, is rusty tin,
But just today we felt the past,
 A horse just wandered in.

*My oldest daughter and her horse Ellie.*

## When an Old Chair Whispers

Askew, it sat upon the porch
Thru summer, heat and frost,
A leg was broke, was all thread bare,
The cushion long since lost.
Nettles have grown thru the floor,
The house beyond repair,
But oh the stories it could tell,
This rumpled, old porch chair.

I stood beside the torn arm,
Weary from my walk,
Closed my eyes to catch my
breath
When it began to talk.
The voice, it seemed a misty thing
(soft words that once were
caught)
But as I ponder it again,
Perhaps it was a thought.
I saw a woman sitting there,
Her hair brushed out, cascade,
I heard her recite scripture
As the light began to fade.
I saw the years that plodded on,
The spring and summer scorch
And saw the day they hauled it
out
And left it on the porch.

68

An old man sat and bowed his head,
Was just at eventide
And thru the mist of all the years,
I listened as he cried.
The chair, once new, had held his life,
Now fewer left to hold,
Both faced the death of unconcern,
Both ragged, worn and old.
The pictures stopped, my thoughts were still,
I studied what was there,
A life of memories scattered 'bout
Like parts of that old chair.

# When Growth Steals

I once had acres out in front,
The fields were to my side,
I watched o're groves of pecan trees,
I was the family's pride.
When fancy horses pranced the road
That led them to my door,
So many things have changed since then,
So different than before.
The sheep were loosed a day or two,
They kept my vast yard cropped,
So often limbs from giant oaks
Were trimmed lest any dropped.
The swing was full upon my porch,
I'd watch the children play,
But now it seems they all have grown
And all have moved away.
The mules have stood out in the shade
And rubbed upon that tree,
Though years have passed since I've seen them
I always try to see
If horse and buggy, mule and plow
Would come a time or two.
I've waited patient thru the years
For them to come in view.
But all I saw were fields sold,
My crops were over run,
The tilled land that I used to know

Laid idle in the sun.
They put in roads where trees once grew,
It felt like such a theft,
My groves, my fields had disappeared,
With houses right and left.

*Melrose*

My porch swing sits with broken chain,
It's not been used in years,
When pavement came, it changed it all,
It's traffic now, one hears.
They let me keep a bit of yard,
I still have shaded grass,
Instead of prancing horses now,
I watch the traffic pass.
They've inched and inched more every year,
Built closer, no regard
For all I've given for their roads,
They've left me little yard.
I yearn to see my fields again

But growth has taken o're
And I alone stand proudly here
As I stood years before.
I wonder what my future is,
I try my best to last
And leave a bit of history,
A trace of what has passed.
In years to come when I am gone,
When nothing old is saved,
There will be some that think of me,
Before the world was paved.

## When Someone Cares

There's a special kind of feeling,
A special kind of grace,
When time has stopped the forward march
Around an old home place.
Where trees hold all the secrets
And the mossy limbs are still,
When the 'baccy barn is holding on
And the house still holds until
The years have stolen all the strength
And taken what it can
And no one now remembers when
They heard the screen door slam.
But progress marches quickly on,
It weakens with abuse
And slowly claims what we don't want
And what we do not use.
Perhaps it's spirits that come out,
Take time from standing guard,
And pick up fallen limbs from trees
And mow the greening yard.
But I think though the house is old,
It fights hard to survive,
Descendants of the ones who farmed
Are keeping it alive
And holding unto what they can,
Though time has pushed and shoved,
There's still someone who visits here
And shows that it is loved.

*Bell*

## When The Truth Hurts

I wish that I could tell the tale, get all of it just right,
The howling wind, the driving rain, the gale that came that night.
When thunders rumble shook the walls and lightening danced around,
When all took shelter from the storm, above and underground.
The tree limbs swooped and finally broke and slammed against the house,
A fire started lapping boards, was quickly dunked and doused.
Windows broke against the wind, it pelted now inside,
People, varmints, horse and hound, looked for a place to hide.
The angry wind, like cannon fire, would blow, then calm, a tease,
It took out barns and took out homes and stripped the trees of leaves
It blew till it had blown down, what had been once a home
And walls that stood a hundred years, stood crooked and alone.
The trees were laying on their side, the roof was now caved in,
Took weeks to gather all the stock, some hurt, some dazed, all thin.
I wish that I could tell this tale and all that it implies,
But if I stopped mid storyline, I'd just be telling lies.
Was not a storm that took her out, though she has seen a few,
It fell so slowly thru the years, it happened in plain view.
It's people died or moved away, not meaning any harm
And slowly house began to fall, was turned into a barn.
Hay was stacked within it's walls, in time the metal leaked,
No one took the time to fix, the places that grew weak.
Year by year the rains have come, the wind has whistled thru,

Not ever was a board repaired, no nail or a screw.
They farmed the land around the house, sprayed water on the crop,
Watched the grass grow lush and green and never saw it drop.
And so like all that's gone before, time takes it's yearly toll
And we have lost another piece, of us from long ago.
I stand and ponder, wonder why, we let the past give way,
To all the ugly houses now, that most love to this day.
I let the silence of this place, burn deep within my mind,
Then sadly, slowly walk away and leave this place behind.
Knowing it was not a storm or tree that over turned,
The end came quiet in the night, unloved and unconcerned.

*Bell*

## When Will It Stop

What makes a man decide it's time
To knock down someone's past?
I stare at picture that once was
And know our end is cast.

A pillared home with shaded porch,
So worthy to be saved,
Yet man decides what shall come down
And what will soon be paved.

A graciousness has left our soul,
When history is no more,
When we care not for those who came
In all the years before.

My heart breaks at the very thought,
Of columns crashing down,
Of doors that worked a hundred years
And welcomed those in town.

I think of trees most likely cut
That shaded life within,
I can't forgive man's unconcern,
Nor can't forgive his sin.

How I'd love to walk your halls,
Hear stories you could speak,

My ears would strain to hear the sound
Of every squeak and creak.

A pillared home with shaded porch,
So worthy to be saved,
You stand no more by man's decree,
Our past has now been paved.

*Gulf Hammock*

## When The Welcome Sign Is Not Out

I can almost see the spirits,
Thru wavy glass of time,
I push against the cobwebs
That spiders used to climb.
The trees have fallen quiet,
Their leaves are still, except
The scurry of a lizard
As I started up the step.
The gray of all the old plank walls
Were rough all 'way across
And in the shadows of the porch
Blended with the moss.
An old chair sat there on the floor,
Covered o're in dust,
A door knob that locked years ago,
Eaten 'way by rust.
Yet still it held and kept me out...
Or locked the spirits in,
The windows all were painted shut,
The curtains, old and thin.
I pressed against the wavy glass
And closed my eyes to squint,
But all I left behind me there
Was nose and fingerprint.
I thought I heard a muffled noise,
The faint sound of a scratch,
I tried the doorknob one more time

And heard the click of latch.
I knew right then, as sure as not,
I wasn't wanted here,
This old home place was still a home
And spirits made that clear.
I slowly walked back to the fence,
For hour was getting late,
I stood and studied silver boards,
Then slowly closed the gate.
I thought the fence had kept cows out,
But that and the old key,
Were meant to keep the stranger out
And meant for even me.
My mind took notes as I stood there,
The boards, the rusty tin;
I realized the fence, the lock
Kept all the spirits in.
I smiled and thought I understood,
This home place had its day
And who wants strangers walking in..
I'd want it the same way.
Was then I heard the old door creak,
I turned around to see,
A child, a woman at the door
Looking back at me.
I walked back to the shaded porch,
She motioned me, come in,
Her clothes threadbare and tattered some
They both were whisper thin.
She brushed the dust from off the chair
And tried to hide her frown,
The child held tightly to her dress,
She asked me to sit down.
It was a moment 'for she spoke,

Her voice was soft and low,
She pulled her child close to her
And spoke of long ago.
"He said that he was coming back,
That I should never leave,
Now it's been years since he has left
And everyday I grieve.
My shelves have emptied long ago.
You must think I so rude,
But look around, we've nothing left,
No water, clothes, no food..
You see it was a few years back,
When others just like you
Came and pushed the old door in,
Took all when they were thru.
They rifled thru my dresser there,
Broke canning jars and glass,
When they left, what was left
Was nothing more than trash.
We locked the door and locked the gate
And never had a doubt
That he would come and rescue us,
We never once went out."
I reached out then to touch her hand,
Both bowed their head and knelt
And as my hand touched only air,
And mist was all I felt.
I shuddered at what I had seen
And what my ears had heard.
I sat a moment to recall
The softness of her word.
I knew she would be waiting still,
I never had a doubt,
I locked the door before I left

To keep the strangers out.
I turned just once and locked the gate,
I left her to be free,
I knew the fence and knew the lock
Was meant for even me.

*Bell*

## Weeds, Graves and Horses

The horses graze along the fence,
And stand there in the shade,
Their used to phantoms in the night
And graze there unafraid.
They see the nettles climb the tomb
And watch the slow decay,
Behind the fence their pasture's mowed,
This side in disarray.
Among the slabs that mark the spot,
The years have posed a threat,
Weeds of unconcern have grown,
To prove we fast forget.
And as they graze the ivy creeps
And weedy seeds have spread
And soon no one will ever know,
They eat beside the dead.
But horses know on moonless nights,
When shadows can't be seen,
That only they will see the mist
That rises in between
Forgotten graves of long before,
When living were allowed
And gathered there to say farewell,
Said prayers and heads were bowed.
The mower cuts the horses grass,
Their pasture, quite immense,
While nothings done to mow the past

On this side of the fence.
The rain will come, the storm will howl,
The winter wind will blow
And only horses know the ones
That lie here just below.
The stones are chipped and worn down,
In shades of black and gray,
The fence holds in the well kept side,
The other in decay.
Sometimes the horses lift their heads,
Stare at allotted plot,
For soon they'll be the only ones
That know what man forgot.

*Picture by Shirley Ashley Benson*

## The Reckoning

I saw them all the day they came,
The horse, the logger, both,
Intending there to clear a path
Amidst the forest growth.

The horses leaned and chains pulled tight,
While mules pulled them clear.
I heard the tremble of the ground
Ahead and in the rear.

I watched them ready saws and men,
I felt the axes pound,
And soon I heard the mighty crack
And I lay on the ground.

They pulled me to a clearing near
And stripped away my bark,
And there I lay for many days
Thru morning, noon and dark.

The mules came and dragged me to
A place of saws and cranks
And there amid the shouts of men
They cut me into planks.

Now many months have passed since then,
I hear the hammers pound,
A wagon creaks and slowly stops,
My planks lift off the ground.

I feel them carve against my side,
Then lay me on a floor,
Lifting me, they place with pride
My trim around the door.

Down thru the years I've seen them come,
I've heard the trot, the horn.
My walls have seen the death of some,
The same ones I saw born.

I watched them come so gaily dressed,
I watched the waltz begin
And always I was proud to be
A part where they walked in.

I lived the years so sad and dark,
Watched Missy walk the floor.
I watched the dust of parting men
As they rode off to war.

I felt the hunger of those years
On both side of my walls,
Here Missy leaned against my side
And reads, "Atlanta falls."

Sharecroppers came and tilled the fields,
Plant cotton for a share.
For many years no one has come,
But yesterday an heir

Unlocked my door and walked around
With hammer and a nail,
And there upon the worn door
Placed a sign, 'For Sale.'

My walls have weathered thru the years,
There's windows that have broke,
The fields no longer grow a crop,
Just scattered pine and oak.

Twas late one night the heaven's split,
The whole house felt the jolt,
Dry timbers fought as well they could
Against the lightening bolt.

But soon the fire ravaged hot,
The timbers cracked and burned
And from that night of fiery wrath
No one has since returned.

The door has long been fallen down,
Decayed against its weight,
I strain to keep the pillars strong,
My fluted trim still straight.

The years have slowly marched along
From those of long ago,
But there beyond the hills and fields
I watch the forest grow

And wonder if the time will come,
When someone stands in awe
And thinks of what that tree could be
And gets out chain and saw.

I hope that as their standing there
And pick the favored tree,
They see the beauty of it's past
And one day think of me.

I strain against the mighty wind,
Though walls are old and frail,
I've lived the hot and steamy night,
The hurricane, the gale.

But now I know my time has come,
There's little left to hold.
My timbers have been scorched and burned,
My fluted trim is old.

The pillars stand against the years,
I know they are the crown
And soon the welcome place I hold
Will all be fallen down.

Until the time that death pulls me
Into a decayed heap,
I'll stand my watch as I had done
While Missy was asleep.

Perhaps when there's a restless night
And sleep will come no more,
You'll think of timbers hewn just right
And trim around my door.

## A Walk Around An Old Home

Amid the dapples of the trees,
It peaks beneath the limbs,
It hides the secrets of it's youth,
Grows old and withered grim.

The windows let the pelting rain
Cover floor and wall
And leaves of fifty years or more
Are silent as they fall.

The chimney stands, though not so straight,
I strain to smell the smoke,
As tangled weeds and ivy crawls
And does it's best to choke.

The weathered boards have turned to gray,
Not ready to be gone,
Knowing well it's time has come,
Yet fighting to hold on.

But in the hush of times gone by,
I feel I have no choice,
But linger there and filter sounds
Until I hear a voice.

The creak of harness pulls me back,
I see a mule and plow,

I see a woman shelling peas,
She wipes her dripping brow.

What man has hewn all these boards,
What team has cleared the land,
What mighty wind will push against
A home that can not stand?

Could spirits of the ones that passed
Be buried just below,
Holding unto mysteries
From those of long ago?

I gently touch a withered wall
And offer up a prayer
For all of those who will miss out
When it's no longer there.

What will we show the youth one day,
How will they understand
When all our histories fallen down,
Neglect will take the land.

Old house, I hold your memory,
Am glad I took the walk,
Wishing I could see you young
And wishing walls could talk.

Epilogue
Now just a whisper on the breeze,
The fields are tilled and sown,
The trees protect the memories,
A home place now alone.

A heap of boards beneath the shade,
The stories lie beneath,
Pushed aside and piled high,
The last great funeral wreath.

The wagon ruts, now long plowed o're,
New fences line the gate,
And time has claimed the old homestead
As progress sealed her fate.

The dappled shade protects the boards,
Pushed neatly in a pile,
Her memories are not yet burned,
Yet will be in awhile.

And still I hear the fire crack,
It's timbers, dried out wood,
Lapping at the memories
From all the years she stood.

I can see the cinders rising,
In whirlwinds to it's crest,
I pray that heaven shuts the sight
From those who are at rest.

The ones that went on long before,
Carved a living from the ground
And now their home is piled high,
Yet I see them all around.

She holds a dish rag in her hand,
Her face is tanned and grim,
Her bonnet shades her years of work,
The kids all cling to him.

Each time I pass the towering trees,
I slow to look upon
And think how glad I took the time
To visit 'fore it's gone.

I see the planks of years long past,
Now century old debris,
A part of history waits to burn
There piled 'neath the trees.

*Bell*

*Elizabeth Jane Bellamy (Croom) died on her wedding night on May 11,1837 when her wedding dress caught fire. Her husband Samuel Bellamy never remarried and on Dec. 23,1853 ended his life by cutting his throat with a razor.*

## Bride to be

Elizabeth, the bride to be
Was just this side of heaven,
A husband waits, a new home built
In eighteen thirty-seven
Her cheeks were blushed, her eyes were bright,
Her mirrors, gilded gold,
She slipped into her wedding gown,
The night would soon unfold.
Carriages arrived that morn,
From every part of town,
Servants held the prancing horse,
While others helped them down.
The gardens were in rosy bloom,
All grown for this day,
For Elizabeth, the bride to be,
This special day in May.
Verandas were all piled high
With food to eat and drink
And voices soon began to blend
Above the crystal clink.
A toast to Samuel Bellamy,
The dashing, nervous groom,

All milled about and waited there
Amidst the roses bloom.
The maids had waited long enough,
One and all agree,
Elizabeth could now walk out,
The lovely bride to be.
Vows were said, he lightly kissed,
(now husband, not a beau)
Friends and kin would celebrate
That night so long ago.
Servants summoned, cleared the room,
All readied for the ball,
As darkness covered gardens,
Chairs were moved against the wall.
Candles flickered, giving light,
Set scene for this romance,
The music slowed, the waltz began,
He held her for this dance.
His hand held snugly at her waist,
She lowered eyes, polite,
This home, her friends, the lovely gown
Were all for her tonight.
No one knew her gossamer gown
Had brushed the candle's glow
And no one knew the bride's first night
was the last she'd ever know.
Servants came with water pail,
Her voice could not be heard,
Her spirit left the pillared home,
No guest could say a word.
Elizabeth, the bride to be,
With mirrors gilded gold,
Samuel spent not one night there
And soon the mansion sold.

A hundred years, plus thirty more,
The home fought hard to stand,
But now it seems it's not worth much,
The dollars' in the land.
I wonder when they knocked it down
And pillars all caved in,
Did spirits of the bride and groom
Decide to stay within
And for a moment have a dance,
'tween ladies and the men
And waltz together one more time
And think what might have been.

*"Yankees have developed a character so odious that death would be preferable to reunion with them." Gov John Milton*

## Governor John Milton

The rooms of Sylvania Mansion
Didn't know he would arrive,
Nor did it know that history
Would change in sixty-five.
For Marianna was not far
From Tallahassee walls
And could not see our governor
Pacing thru it's halls.
He knew that word was coming,
The South would taste defeat,
Rumors swirled within, without,
Down Tallahassee streets.
Yank blockades were in our ports,
We hung on by a thread
And pushed them back to make a way
To keep our soldiers fed.
But word was coming in a day,
Or two or maybe three,
That Grant had papers drawn up,
To sign by General Lee.
The South lay burned and smoking still,
By yank's insane desire,
What yankee could not steal or kill,

They left behind on fire.
And thru it all, Milton paced,
Boots echoed on the floor,
He called for horse and carriage
To be brought up to the door.
He lingered there a moment
And slowly shook his head,
Thinking of long months before,
Of all the Southern dead.
Marianna called to him,
He knew he'd take a stand,
That he would never see the day,
A yank would take his land.
He left the governor's mansion,
The South would not survive
And so he left the capital,
That day in sixty-five.
Sylvania Mansion was his home
And under rising sun,
The Governor, with steadfast hand
Cocked hammer on his gun.
With one quick shot, he proved his point,
As blood began to pool,
Said death was more preferred than that
Of having yankee rule.
Sylvania never was the same,
For years it held the cloak,
Of suicide and blood stained floor,
It too went up in smoke.
A little sign now marks the spot,
Keeps history alive
And very few will hear the shot
From eighteen sixty-five.
A hundred years, plus fifty more

Have proved the Governor's fear,
Surrender signed, yankee rule
And now they all live here.
Condos, malls, restaurants galore,
Strange dialects from the mouth,
I think to myself, Milton was right
While we save what is left of the South.
The Governor's Mansion, torn down,
Sylvania, an old episode
And all that is left is a little sign
That marks where it was on the road.

*Two Egg*

# Rowdy

The sun had not yet streaked the sky,
Before they came for me,
Harness down and wagon hitched
We left from Tennessee.
We plodded miles from mountain top,
Crossed rivers, creeks and bogs,
Master stopped to shoot a deer,
Got lucky with the hogs.
The miles crept on, the wagon creaked,
Past laurel, oak and pine,
We stopped that night for prayer and rest,
Then crossed the Florida line.
The skeeters bit from morn till nite,
The gnats ate at my ears,
My legs grew weary from the weight
But I just persevered
And we moved onward to the south,
Most twenty miles a day,
The wagon ruts were not so deep,
But awful in the clay.
The children jumped unto the ground,
They played, I heard them squeal
And master climbed from off the seat,
Put shoulder to the wheel.
We made it there, I got my rest,
But much is left to do,
Wood to mill, fields to clear,

Where only brambles grew.
The master had me hauling logs,
But Bertie would run out,
In quiet moments she would sit
And tell me all about
The bedroom that she soon would have,
The stall that would be mine
And often she would braid my mane
With honeysuckle vine.
I saw the house grow day by day,
Plowed fields for a crop,
Saw wild flowers by the creek,
And had no time to stop.
But now the years have passed so quick,
Most my hair is gray,
But Bertie still comes out to me
And shoo's the flies away.
The houses now have come so close,
There's more than one in sight
And often when I wake from sleep
I see electric light.
I wonder what comes down the road
At nite and in the morn
And stops out front, delivers mail
And blows that awful horn.
My time has come to work no more,
My knees are stiff and bent,
I slowly walk to farthest field
To help and to prevent
Miss Bertie seeing me lie down
For I could not ignore
All her cries to keep me here
For I can do no more.
I lift my head and see the home,

One last time, my eyes clear
And now I'm told there is a cross
That says, "Rowdy lies here."
And twined around my wooden cross,
An elegant design,
Of wild flowers by the creek
And honeysuckle vine.

L-R David Moore Family -- Rowdy the horse, Jennie, Sarah, David Moore, Georgia, Bertie (with doll), Lena Creary. Greenwood 1885

## The Reunion

The ghosts that live within these walls
Are not about to rid,
The memories of all they know,
That jealously they've hid.

But yet they call me to this place
And beckon me inside,
How gracious are the spirits here
They've chosen for my guide.

They take me slowly room by room,
Like players that are cast
And I become like one of them,
A captive in the past.

I let the smell of dank and dust
Fill me in and out,
I feel their presence ever near
And slowly look about.

I see past all the charred decay
Where fire lapped the wall,
And marvel at the splintered doors
That lead from off the hall.

There in a far off corner
Away from years of junk,

I kneel and touch the iron clasp
That opens up a trunk.

I feel the spirits steady gaze,
I know they've gathered 'round,
I hesitate, my breath has stopped
Amazed at what I found.

I touch the collar's frilly lace,
The folded dress beneath
And smell the flowers neatly placed
And pinned there in a wreath.

I hold the dress up to myself,
To beautiful to wear,
Then slowly slip into it's folds,
Put flower wreath in hair.

The clouded mirror in the room
Has quickly disappeared,
The floor length image by the trunk
Is clean and now has cleared.

In just a glance the house has changed,
There's no decay, no gloom
And music playing from below
Has pulled me from this room.

A stranger there in coat of gray,
Stood handsome, dashing, grand,
He bowed and smiled and walked to where
I stood and took my hand.

We waltzed and whirled into the night
With fiddles and guitars,
We walked among the gardens there
And kissed beneath the stars.

I felt  the house embracing me,
It's spirits intertwined,
I watched the stranger riding off
Till he was just outlined

Against the ghostly shadows
Of a mossy covered limb
And thru the darkness of the past
I cried and called to him.

I kneel beside the wooden trunk
And touch the satin, lace,
I close my eyes to pull him back,
Remembrance of his face.

I feel the spirits leading me,
A grave that's marked unknown,
With C.S.A. carved just beneath
And my name carved in stone.

I touch the name that I am called,
Now living and alive,
Yet my death year carved in stone
Is eighteen sixty five.

How can I leave now that I know
These things I can't ignore.
The spirits lead me to the trunk
I'd packed long years before.

I've watched the moon rise many years,
I've grown old and thin,
I've never left the mansion house
Since when I entered in.

But just tonight the music plays,
The waltz is soft and slow,
I'll walk the stairs just one more time,
For he is there below.

The spirits now have added one,
I think there'll be no more,
He and I have come back home
And spirits locked the door.

## Roll The Years Back

It wasn't very long ago,
Before the plane and bus,
Before the Wal-Mart's over built,
Before the yanks found us;
That time had kissed our Southern ground,
Heard no such thing as sprawl,
Our neighbors were most likely kin
And we still said, "Y'all."

When porches were a resting place,
Shell limas, black eyed peas,
When one road, maybe now was paved

For chugging Model T's.
I thank the Lord, he's saved a few
Towns from growing pains,
There's still a few old tree lined roads
That once were country lanes.
Now to this day I'll take a walk
When things get way to fast,
And let a picture talk to me,
Then step into the past.

## Limbs, Trails and an Old House

I've sat beside the old, dirt road
When it was just a trail,
I've seen the deer, bobcat and coon
And watched the tiny quail.
The tree limbs were not quite that large
When they began to spread,
The road was just a narrow path
That widened up ahead.
Thru all these years I've stood in place,
Unwavered by the load,
Of  how the time so quickly passed,
As I sat by the road.
The silence of these many years
Does not have its rewards,
My roof now leaks and lets in rain,
While termites eat my boards.
My windows are left open now,
To me it seems unfair,
That time goes on despite the fight
I've fought against despair.
I watch the limbs come closer now,
Much like a mourner's veil,
What shaded children playing then
Now shade a dusty trail.
When I am gone perhaps they'll speak
Or someone write an ode,
Of when I was a stately home
That sat beside the road.

## Old and Hallowed Place

I slowly walk upon the planks of those that went before,
I see their heads bowed deep in prayer, some kneeling on the floor.
A child is hushed and quickly kissed, a young boy gets a glare,
My ears have heard the whispers, of faint and loving prayer.

*Ellzey Methodist Church*

How many words of praise have soared, to rafters up above,
from Satan's hellish brimming pool, to God's undying love?
Cathedrals, he has built himself, with mountains, tree and sky
And nothing man could ever build, would ever testify
To his glory evermore, for we were at a loss;
I look above the pulpit there and eyes fall on a cross.

A wooden beam, not hewn smooth, above the dirt and mud,
It trickled down and made a pool, heaven's saving blood.
He could have called out Satan, destroyed both he and pride.
He could have had ten thousand men and angels at his side.
Yet there he stayed thru out the day, while others cursed, blapheme,
While every moment blood pulsed out and stained the wooden beam.
The Romans and Centurions, had thought he died in shame,
But from the cross it trickled down and fell upon my name.
For he is here, I feel his touch, his Spirit fills this place,
I bow my head, I bend my knees and thank him for his grace.
Thru centuries of war and peace, from birth, death, to the graves,
The cross on walls from old to new reminds me, Jesus Saves.

# On A Walk

The afternoon was waning, the hour was getting late,
When walking down a dusty road, I saw a rusted gate.
The trees had grown 'round the fence and brambles twined
between,
Yet roses pushed thru fallen fence, thru tangled ivy green.
I stopped to pick a tiny rose, that grew in sunny patch
And wondered at the brambles that held to rusty latch.
There were no signs to warn me, to tell me, must stay out
And so I climbed the rusted fence to take a look about.
Far back into the corner, were tombstones, chipped away,
Another lay there on it's side, moss covered in decay.
The granite slab had cracked apart and ivy reached within,
I pulled the brambles from the stone, while briars pulled my skin.
So strong they held, with mighty grip, they covered up the shame;
Each tombstone had the C.S.A., but none revealed a name.
Forgotten in some planted trees, that grew so much the higher,
To shade the graves of those forgot that lay beneath the briar.
I knelt and touched the cold, gray stone, where names all should
have been,
I offered up a prayer to God and prayed for Southron men.
The stones, so cold and crumbled now, cracked and torn apart,
A monument to unconcern, some mother's broken heart.
Yet ivy knows who lies below and trees give shade within,
While strangers pass and never see the rose that covers sin.
For apathy has come this way, another episode,
In caring not for what we've lost, down dusty, southern road.

## This Home Is Now For Sale

One day as I went walking,
In the autumn's windy cold,
I wandered down a worn path
That left the winding road.

*Trenton*

The woods were very quiet
And smelled of tainted leaves,
Surprised, I saw a shadow
Of a house amidst the trees,
A 'For Sale' sign hung on the door

With an old man sitting there.
"Go right on in and look around,"
He told me from his chair.
"The kids took most of Momma's things,
What's left is very old,
A bureau here, a rocking chair,
A blackened, antique stove.
For years the stove has warmed me
And now that I'm alone,
My kids have all forgot me
And this place just don't seem home.
Just feel free to look around
And take your time inside.
I don't get visitors much these days,
In fact, since Momma died.
My kids, their all to busy
To come 'round here no more,
My daughter runs a beauty shop,
My son he owns a store.
My kids both have their families
And big homes down in town.
They're much to busy with their lives
To ever come around.
So everything's for sale,
The house and all within,
Takes more than walls to make a house
A home worth livin' in."
And as I watched this kindly man,
Alone, just sitting there.
I realized how time goes by
And  thought his kids unfair.
He must have read my saddened eyes,
For then I heard him say,
"Kids are only lent to you,

Till you send them on their way.
Letting go is always hard,
Kids make it on their own,
Then suddenly you're sitting here,
Reliving times alone.
When all to soon the sound you hear,
Is hammer on the nail,
And on the door you place the sign,
This home is now for sale."

# Critters and Unconcern

The years have weathered every part
And hastened your decay,
Time rusts metal on your roof
And turned your boards to gray.
It's twisted cypress and the pine,
Time was not your friend,
The raindrops of a thousand storms
Has brought about your end.

*Trenton*

I wonder if someone had stayed
And lived within your walls
And kept the lanterns trimmed and full

As evening darkness falls,
Would critters all have stayed away,
and nails be hammered back,
A watchful eye and constant work
Would stop this time attack.
But holes where windows used to be
Now let the critters in,
The dying folks and unconcern
Is where it will begin.
The fields are tilled, yet plowed around
The house and near the trees
And soon the weeds will cover o're
The past and house debris.
Each thunder clap and howling wind
Will push against your side,
The owl leaves, the coon peeks out
And mice hide there inside.
There must be someone that was loved,
That called this house their own,
That swept the floor and shelled the peas
And made this house a home.
Now battered boards have pulled away,
Warped and fallen down
And soon the home will not hold on,
Mere rubble on the ground.
I slow each time I pass you by,
Each time your more unfit,
Yet standing still there under limbs,
I marvel at your grit.
Please rest well from all your years,
Time takes what we allow,
The others have moved on or died,
Your home to critters now.

# The Brambles, the Bed and the Road

I pushed thru all of the brambles
That pulled at legs and shin.
I fought the winter nettles
That grabbed and bloodied skin.
There behind an old wire fence,
A clearing in the trees.
I thought at first it was a heap
Of pushed up farm debris.
But there it stood, still hanging on,
The porch all rotted through,
Windows long since given up,
It's floor and walls askew.
Not a thing was left behind,
Just bed springs, rusty, frail,
Not a shred of evidence
To help me tell it's tale.
I leaned a moment on the porch
And listened to the birds
And ran my fingers cross the stairs,
Was then I heard his words.
"I plowed the fields and tilled the ground,
Like those before me done,
Put pasture in for mule and cow,
Put hay up by the ton."
I sat there quiet as the breeze
Blew around my face,
Chatter from the birds had stopped,

118

Just quiet in their place.
I thought the man had left me there,
I stood to start my walk,
But gentle breeze was spirit wind
And he began to talk.
"You see the road there through the trees,
The one that led you here?
Used to be a trail years back,
For horse, for hog and deer.
It used to be my way to town,
But things were slower then.
The wagon creaked, got stuck in ruts,
But that was way back when
We went to town but once a month,
Took nearly a full day.
The county came and called it theirs,
A thing called, Right of Way.
Soon the asphalt paved my trail,
A straight line now to town,
The county claimed another lane
And tore my fences down.
It wasn't long before I was
To old to work so hard
And spent my hours raking leaves,
An old man in his yard.
Was then the weeds began to sprout,
The woods grew thick and dense
And nettles soon began to spread
And grow along the fence.
My bed was in the parlor,
I never had a doubt
That I would ever see the day
That I did not walk out."
The air again was quiet,

The breeze no longer blew.
I strained to hear his voice again,
But I knew he was through.
I stayed a few more moments
And pondered this affair,
Was then I heard him shut the door,
But there was no door there.
Black Angus now graze in his field,
The county changed it's code,
Barb wire stretches post to post
And follows asphalt road.
The house fights bravely to hold on,
It's standing, yet somehow,
I wonder if the old man knows
He sleeps on bed springs now.
I slowly walk thru brambles bite,
Protecting cracker shack.
I know I heard the front door shut,
But I do not look back.

*Bell*

## Gateway To the Sky

I still remember all the creaks,
The whippoorwills, the heat,
The frosty nights, the many steps,
Cold treads beneath my feet.
But as a child, the many steps
Were not this steep nor high.
I played upon each worn tread,
My castle to the sky.
They say my granddad cut the tree
And milled the wood himself
And fashioned it to tables, stairs
And cut the cupboard shelf.
The square cut nails that he used
Can still be clearly seen.
The memories come flooding back
As I look through the screen.
The handle on the old screen door
Is rusted, worn thin.
It's screen has long since blown away,
So slowly I walk in.
I lean and touch a worn stair,
Transported back in time;
When I was just a little kid
And they weren't hard to climb.
I saw my dolls all neatly placed
Along the highest stair
And for a moment all those passed

Were standing 'round me there.
These were the stairs my daddy climbed,
His arm around a wife.
I saw the mark my brother left,
When he got his first knife.
From in the shadows Grandma called,
Her hair held by one comb.

*McCulley Farms*

They all were standing on the stairs
To welcome me back home.
In just an instant they were gone
Into the coming dark.
I ran my hand across the spot

That held my brother's mark.
My knees creaked like the worn stairs,
I climbed a few, would stop;
It took me so much longer now
Before I reached the top.
We had no railing way back then,
We took steps two by two,
Now steps were steadied by the wall,
Like I'd seen Grandma do.
I will admit to teary eyes
As slowly I came down,
Balanced by the old blue wall,
Now stained and dirty brown.
I stood a minute at the door.
Old times and those between
Flew through my mind in moments
Like the tatters of the screen.
A hundred years the staircase stood
And I can testify
This was the place that grounded me,
My gateway to the sky.

# Through Hope and Sadness

I sit and ponder why it is, a house just has no glory;
A house takes years to make a home, takes livin' for it's story.
It needs the cries of babies born, of worn staircase tread;
It needs the toys of youthful kids, it even needs the dead.
But soon as someone hears the tale, of something in it's past,
Then one by one they pass it by, all fearful and aghast.
But some say murder within walls, will write it's epithet,
And buyers pass the storied house, until the years forget.

*Inglis*

And so the house begins to fall, it fights against decay,
And buyers shirk at low cost price and run the other way.
They say there is no stainless steel, no open floor plan there,

124

They point out peeling walls and such and call it a nightmare.
A home that has 100 years, not made for those today;
You buy the new, leave us the old, complainers go away.
I will listen to it's stories, the good ones and the bad;
I'll listen to what ever ghosts, will tell, the good and sad.
No home is ever just a house, the walls, the roof, the stairs,
Will tell the time of long past years, to anyone that cares..
All the lives of those that lived and died will be it's story,
And but a few will take the time, to see the old home's glory.

*This home had several murders take place within it's walls and sat vacant, with a low price tag. Someone has now bought it and hopefully will restore it to it's former glory.*

## The Day Journey

I sit here looking at a page, without a thought in sight.
I'm ready for a journey and wonder what to write.
I find a favored photograph, somewhere I can begin,
And listen to the tale it tells, then slowly I walk in.
I've walked thru dappled sunlight, thru the battleground of smoke,
Today it's under mossy limbs of century gnarled oak.
I let my mind conjure up, take over the contrast
Of yesteryears and today and step into the past.
The sadness of another time, of satin and of lace,
Have pulled me from the shadow's near, till I have found this
place.
The pillared porch is holding back the shadows of the morn,
The floor now creaks beneath my feet, splintered, old and worn.
The paint has peeled, the termites eat and hurry the decay,
The memories within, without, have long since gone away.
I gently push against the door, it's hinges pocked with rust,
The air is thick from many years, things covered o'er in dust.
Framed pictures lay against the wall, a husband and a wife,
Surrounded by someone's neglect, forgotten in this life.
A baby's buggy in the hall, it's top is torn, askew,
If I believed there could be ghosts, I'd say there's here a few.
I wiped the cobwebs from the man, then let my fingers slide,
To painted canvas next to him, a young and lovely bride.
Three children in a ghostly pose, captured in three stares,
It all cried out in loneliness, how is it no one cares?
I climb up to the landing, then unto second floor,
Adding up the cost it'd take to get this all restored.

How many stories could it tell, were they waiting there for me?
Was then I heard the giggle, one child, then two, then three.
I looked around, but not one thing, was there to make a sound,
The dusty light that filtered thru was the only thing around.
Yes, if I believed in ghosts, I'd say there's here a few,
Old pictures leaning on the wall downstairs would be a clue.
I left them there within the walls, they each had guarding posts,
I guess I could have stayed and talked, if I believed in ghosts.

# At the Cross

I wonder when God knew the seed
Had touched the hallowed ground;
Were angels gathered all about
To hear the seedling sound?

*Fort White*

The heaven's rain has watered it,
From days when it was small,
The sun has nurtured all the leaves
To something now so tall.
The mighty roots grew thru the years

And anchored it in place,
The mighty tree would change the world
From law unto his Grace.
But as it grew, no one could know
That soon one would be slain,
That blood would cover all man's sins
From now and back to Cain.
Did heaven hear the striking ax
From all those years ago?
The tree that God had slowly grown
Was cut down here below.
And hewn into mighty pole,
Removing bark and moss,
With rusty nails and ragged rope
Was fashioned in a cross.
Now who's to know how many lives
Were taken on it's beam
And who can know the anguish there,
The blood, the cries, the scream?
But one was coming, yet unknown,
The world had no clue,
A sinless Savior, Son of God,
Believed in by a few.
They held their trial, mocked the man,
The whip was made to crack,
They spat upon the Son of Man,
Drew blood across his back.
They pounded nails into his wrists,
Bound hands and nailed feet;
While Satan smiled and thought he won,
That death would be complete.
But as the cross was lifted high,
It shuttered as it slammed,
And there Christ was, our sacrifice,

Unspotted, Holy Lamb.
His blood dripped down his arms, his legs,
In rivulets down his face,
From sacrificial offerings
To God's undying Grace.
He looked ahead through all the years
Past my mistakes and shame,
While he was on the cross that day
His blood fell on my name.
For hours there across the beam
Was God's begotten Son,
And Satan smiled, believing that
He at last had won.
But Christ, the perfect Lamb of God
Would not leave us alone,
The blood that seeped upon the ground
Was now before the throne.
Remission of my many sins
Will never mark my loss,
For that was settled years ago
At the foot of the Savior's cross.

# At the Water's Edge

She lay so quiet in her grief, first days, a month, a year,
Her mind so troubled most the time, for minutes it would clear.
Her youthful years were wasted here, she stared at ceiling, walls
And spoke of when he kissed her there, a young man lean and tall.
She'd whisper, "Please come back to me," we'd hold her hand and pray,
She'd kiss the ring he gave to her, before he rode away,
But mostly she lay quiet, still and no one ever heard,
What battleground he fought upon, no letter, sight nor word.
And there remained our little belle, for days, for months, a year,
Then one day came the whispered words she must never hear.
Ten miles away Ocean Pond was stained with southron red
And no one thought she ever heard a word that parents said.
For days, for months, then finally years, we kneeled there to pray
And could not tell her that her love had died ten miles away.
Her auburn hair has turned to white, her fingers held the ring
And thru the years we never thought she ever heard a thing.
Then late one night she called them in, told servants soft and low,
To get the buggy right out front, she had somewhere to go.
She bound them to her silence, an oath to never tell,
They helped her up to buggy seat, she bid them a farewell.
She slapped the reins against the horse, her hands were weak and frail.
The moonlight beams fell all around her wedding gown and veil.
The mare took a step then stopped and gave a feeble neigh,
She slapped the reins to start the trip, a pond ten miles away.
The buggy bumped along the road, while servant sat beside,

A woman with her withered hands, dressed up to be a bride.
With halting steps he helped her down, from off the buggy seat,
She leaned on him to get her there,  there would be no retreat.
He gasped a breath as she stepped in, she shook his hand away
And he knew then she heard the words in whispers from that day.
The water now was running clean, the years have claimed the dead,
But Lord the color has come back, to cheeks, to hands, to head.
He heard her call, "Come back to me," was more than he could stand,
He reached for her, but now she held fresh flowers in her hand.
That's more than fifty years ago, her story has been told,
Been passed around and passed on down till all have grown old.
Her bed has stayed untouched, unmade, a beauty and her beau,
No one has entered thru the doors she left so long ago.
Lovers now come to the spot, pick flowers at their peak,
Flowers from a bride's bouquet now grow along the creek.
So many walk beside the pond where southron men have died,
And often tell of auburn hair with soldier by her side.
Her room is waiting patiently in case there comes a day,
He carries her back in his arms, from just ten miles away.

# The Ballad of the McNeill Home

They called me a Grand old Lady,
People would walk and greet,
Under the century trees out front,
On sidewalks of Robinson Street.
I watched as children were born,
Three, then four and then five,
The bedrooms were full of wee little folks
And all of my rooms were alive.
Those years, my halls knew just laughter,
Verandas were long and wide,
So many socials under my roof,
People in here and outside.
My shutters would hold back the gales,
That blew in from off of the lake
And Miss Mary would hum thru the thunder
That kept all the children awake.
At night Miss Mary would cover
Her shoulders, with old knitted shawl
And soon you would hear her bow on the strings
From her violin kept in the hall.
My timbers held in the music,
My floors felt the tapping of feet
And the years seem to pass way to quickly
For those on East Robinson Street.
Miss Mary had now lost two husbands
And two of her children had died,
Loneliness now has filled up my rooms
And emptied my porch, long and wide.

Both I and Miss Mary were aging
And time is often unkind,
My beauty was waning a wee little bit,
Miss Mary was now going blind.
I'd watch her sit at the table
And pen out poem after poem.
Of days yet to come and those that have passed
When laughter was heard in this home.
Now she stays in an upstairs bedroom,
In a daybed by window seat,
Her eyes have been robbed of the sunlight
That shines down on Robinson Street.
But a child now sits at her bedside
And Mary no more is alone,
Miss Mary calls her, 'My Flower Face,"
This child of a child of her own.
I watched as her breathing grew shallow,
She would no more feel the heat,
Nor the wind that blew off of the water
In back of East Robinson Street.
I watched them take my Miss Mary,
The day was cloudy and warm,
I recited the poem I once watched her write,

> ### *"The Calm That Comes After The Storm*
> *The storms of life passed o'er me*
> *And left me unafraid,*
> *The wrongs by others done me,*
> *The errors I have made*
> *Have all been left behind me*
> *And days of sweet content*
> *Repay me now a thousand fold*
> *For troubled days I've spent."*

My great halls were now quiet,
No children, no kin of kin,
It startled my slumber the day that I saw
All the men and the trucks driving in.
They pulled at my windows and shutters,
Took porches and chimneys down,
Pulled floorboards my children had walked on
And scattered me all thru the town.
Some think I'm gone and forgotten,
All seem to be looking ahead.
Now towering buildings with stories of glass
Is what they have built there instead.
No porches to beckon the neighbors,
No hallways to welcome inside,
Century old trees have given their space
For roadways, to busy and wide.
Porches and pillars have all been replaced,
Men call the past obsolete,
But Miss Mary and I know the beauty once there
When we both lived on Robinson Street.

Family home of Lyn Augustine Chilton. The poem *The Calm Comes After The Storm*, written by Miss Mary Lide.

*Orlando*

135

# The Final Step

Today I sit beneath the trees and rest neath all it's shade,
The shovel there atop the mound has fallen as I prayed.
I ponder at this weedy plot and think of all the years;
An old man now, but once I was a Florida volunteer.
We fought so hard to hold our ground, to build that wooden
bridge.
Now eyes are dim, I barely see from high atop this ridge.
And though my ears hold muffled sound, I still can hear their cry,
I hear the balls crash thru the trees, the arms, the chest, the thigh.
Was more than fifty years or so, but battle din is loud,
Thru all the years that's passed since then, my head was never
bowed
And only then to say a prayer for strength to carry on,
Now here I sit in weedy field where friends were killed upon.
I slowly let thoughts wander back when smoke filled all the air,
When wild hogs had their fill, this field was burnt and bare.
The cries of fallen fill my ear while cannonade explode,
No ambulance could get on thru the wooded, rutted road.
But thru the years I've tried my best to clear the rock, the stone,
I've farmed the fields, loved a wife, made trees into a home.
But living here in whispered past has kept the ghosts alive,
They've stayed with me all thru the years and helped me to survive
The death of wife, of daughter, son, to see the brambles grow,
To watch a home in disrepair, the river over flow.
I wonder who will walk the path long after I have left,
And will they know what happened here for time is surely theft
And steals all the memories of those that's gone before,

While weeds and trees cover land that knows the cost of war.
I know it's time for me to go, and slowly look about,
The gray clad soldiers call to me with arms all reaching out.
I hesitate for one last look, the fields, the house, the war.
I say a prayer, "Remember here," and slowly I step o're.

*Near the Santa Fe River*

## A Walk In The Dark

Good grief, the weather really stinks,
Rain misty, sky is gray,
It's warm within and cold without,
I think I'll go away.
There's dusty roads just to my left,
A path just to my right,
The dusty road is dark and dank,
The other bathed in light.
And now I think which one to choose,
What mood might I be in.
Ha, what a joke it is to me,
I quietly begin.
The tree limbs sweep and hug the road
And call me to embark.
I push aside the hanging moss
And step into the dark.
Soon the breeze is blowing cold,
The tree limbs lean and sway,
The dusty road I'm walking down
Is dank, is dark and gray.
My mind begins to whisper things,
I think I hear a voice;
And as I walk, I'm wondering
What made me make this choice.
I always pick the run-down home,
With peeling paint and grime,
I pass the ones that's bathed in light

For those that transgress time.
She called to me and led me here,
Now stretches out her hands,
Her misty shadow welcomes me,
Her shack just barely stands.

A candle flickers on the sill,
No window has a screen,
There's just a chair against the wall,
The floors have been swept clean.
She lets me see what she has known,
No words and no remark,
Yet I could see down thru her years,
There sitting in the dark.
But pelting rain has called me back,
I've never left my chair,

Her memories have claimed my time
Though I was never there.
One day the path that I will choose
 will likely be my last
And someone else will pick my road
And listen to my past.
Now what a joke I tell myself,
I've nothing good to show,
No pillared mansion, fancy grave,
Something from long ago.
My stories are from other's thoughts,
I live their episodes,
That must be why I choose the path
That leads down darkened roads.

# A Shady Lane

I was sitting on a park bench, under early spring time blooms,
Shaded by the willow trees, while oaks draped over tombs.
The greatest of our fair, young men, had lived thru war and grief,
Now here I sat beneath the shade, while they lay underneath.
I wander down the winding lanes, part paved, part sand, part clay
And gently touch the chiseled stone, some fancy, plain, all gray.
A tiny stone with chiseled words, marked only with a year,
Was then I pushed the leaves aside, "A Drummer Boy Rests Here."
I prayed for all our Southron men, that lay beneath the sod
And feel the bitter pain of those, known only to our God.
The peaceful place I came upon, was loud and now askew,
Scattered parts of men and mule have come into my view.
I come across a line of ants, I watch them one by one,
And wonder if this battlefield, is where they have begun.
I now can see their great, long line, starting frenzied deed,
Crawling up the trouser leg, as soldiers start to bleed.
I hear the flies begin to buzz, 'round parts that are exposed,
They and ants begin to feed 'round eyes that never closed.
From high up in the treetops, the vultures on alert,
Lest any part of any man, go uncovered in the dirt.
The shovels scrape against the rock, the holes are twenty wide,
As soldiers bleed and die from wounds, we place them side by
side.
When evening comes we mark for them, the places where they lay.
I place the drum upon the mound, for he will never play.
I jump ahead six months or more, the war is finally o'er,
And granite tombs now mark the place, of crosses there before.

The drum lays now in pieces, I gather what I can,
And place them on his granite tomb, this boy, not yet a man.
No name is known for this  child, that's buried 'neath the oak,
Maneuvers are now silent, drums frayed and sticks now broke.
I see a hawk hang high above, he's ready for attack,
But bones have long since turned to dust, his screech now calls me
back.
I see again the line of ants, my heart begins to roar,
I start to squash them neath my feet, but stop and I step o'er.
Then faintly as I walk away, leave shade for summer heat,
I hear the haunting echo, of a fife and drummer's beat.
I turn to look, is no one there, but markers, straight and plumb
And 'round the unmarked grave of one, are braids from off  his
drum.

## A Shady Place in a Field

I always turn to take a look
And slow as I drive by,
I stare into the shaded place,
I guess to verify
The sadness that I feel within,
How hard to now appease
The gloomy shadows of my thoughts..
The waste beneath the trees.
Several times I've turned around
And did not hesitate,
I've walked in, while you were there,
Before your fence and gate.
I should have known when posts were set
And tractors plowed the ground,
For when the wire was all pulled tight
They came and pulled you down.
Did they hear the past call out,
Did they see your grace,
For now the ghosts in ragged rooms
Have all been now displaced.
And history was taken down,
An empty plot their prize,
How often I have looked your way....
No reason for demise.
I did not get a single board
From all the years you stood,
No chimney brick, no broken glass,

No nail, no shard of wood.
I did not know one day I'd pass
And like a reprobate,
Who's sin was time and unconcern......
I stand here at your gate.
But gates and fence can not keep out,
Nor heavy corner posts
Can not contain the whispers there,
Of all the displaced ghosts.
For no reprieve will ever come,
Remembrance will fade
And history is now a part
Of tractors in your shade.

*Bell*

## The Immigrant

A trunk with leather straps to hold, against the thief and crew,
The bits and pieces of our lives, part me, our son and you.
I so remember how the waves would send their salty spray,
Across the bow, it gushed on by, amid it's disarray.
For many weeks we prayed the stars, be out at eventide,
We prayed their brightness in the dark, would shine and be our guide.
You tried to smile when we saw land, though journey made you frail,
With arms around your son and I, we stood beneath the sail.
This place of freedom beckoned us, it's stories, great and grand;
Of flowing rivers, miles of plains and promise of free land.
We settled into boarding house, to stay three days or four,
At night the men in town would talk and whisper of a war.
Just five days past the morning light, when we had left the ship,
My son and I both learned the word and meaning of conscript.
With hardly time for thoughts of home and less time yet to miss,
Our voyage o're the raging sea, had led us here to this.
I knew of distant kinfolk, by way of word of mouth,
I said good-by to frail wife and sent her further south.
For Maryland was grabbing sons, the fine, the poor, the worst,
But front lies needed more and more and immigrants were first.
My son was sent along the coast, he faded from my view,
He and I had come so far, now forced to wear the blue.
So many nights I lay awake and pondered on my life
And prayed so hearty for my son and for my frail wife.
Finally I'd gotten word, when months there wasn't none,

My frail wife was holding on, but we had lost a son.
I thought of her so long ago, when she was but a maid,
When first I held my only child, there in the glen and glade.
But fast my thoughts were pushed aside, amid the smoke and yell,
And tears of loss soon dried my cheek, amid the shot and shell.
How I remember on that morn, they laid me on the floor
And took the leg I walked upon, for me, the war was or'e.
I hobbled southward on my crutch, each step felt like a knife,
Faltering, though they seemed to be, got closer to my wife.
 I neared the shell pocked house at dawn, I prayed God would allow,
A coming home to welcome me, but found a fevered brow.
For she had lingered there a week and talked of ship and sail,
Again she saw the rigging fight against the stormy gale.
She murmured of this freedom land, I cooled her blazing head,
She called her son and called to me and then she lay there dead.
I guess the years have passed on by, these clapboards, old and gray,
Are telling me each passing month, that all have gone away.
I touch the curtains I keep closed, now little more than junk,
I close my eyes and see the day, she laid them in the trunk.
So happy was the day we left, we smiled and waved good-by,
The only free land is the grave, I too, now wait to die.

*Bell*

146

## Let's Go Back

My husband tried to drive on by,
Said something 'bout a shack,
I quickly gave him a bad look,
Turned and pointed back.
He groaned as I stepped from the truck,
He knew he wouldn't win,
I heard him say, "It's almost dark,"
Before I entered in.
Was such a mess, hard to believe
That things were strewn about,
Wiring cut, windows broke,
Busted shelves through out.
I picked my way to tiny room
And pushed against the door,
A few old books, mildewed, wet,
Bed springs upon the floor.
I bent and picked up soggy book
That lay in the debris,
Pages stuck and binding tore,
I held it up to see.
The cover had a faded dog,
The title worn away,
I could not leave this children's book
To vanish in decay.
I held it tight and weaved my way
Thru  home that's now a tomb,
Past broken things that once were new

In each old and damaged room.
I made my way back to the porch
Where I could get a look,
I carefully flipped a page or two
From old and mildewed book.

Crayons had marked a special page,
Was then I found it there,
A worn and faded picture
Of a girl with curly hair.
She was holding to a puppy,
It's tail obscured by wags,
And on the back in colored crayon,
'My best friend, Mr. Rags.'
I slowly walked back to the truck
And stopped a moment till
I could find the strength to turn
And look back up the hill,
To home place that was loved and lost,

It's future bleak and bad,
A home that housed a child and dog
That looked like one I had.
I showed my husband what I found,
He'd never understand
And really showed no interest
In what was in my hand.
I put the picture in a frame,
That held two by design,
A little girl with Mr. Rags
Now rests there next to mine.
Her child's book in plastic bag,
Kept safe from bug attack,
I smile and think of what I've saved
By always going back.

# A Lifetime On A Porch

My old tin ages year to year,
I welcome in the ghosts,
My floorboards sag out on the porch
And bugs now eat my posts.
Now years have taken quite the toll,
And all the years demand,
With all the strength that I have left,
I struggle now to stand.
At night when moonlight filters thru,
The cedars growing near,
I think the voices I once heard
Are once again in here.
I hear the pitch pump, up and down,
The water gurgle forth,
I see the stacks of firewood
As wind blows from the north.
But mostly I remember when
Folks looked on me with pride,
When Granny and a little girl
Shelled peas just right outside.
When water in a cast iron tub
Was deep enough to wade,
And baths were always so much fun
Out under the porch shade.
My memories are calling forth
the years before despair,
When children laughed and men folk talked

And all had nightly prayer.
I watched as they moved most my things
And piled them high outside.
They never knew when it all left,
This old house nearly died.
I hear them when they walk so close,
Could touch me with a hand,
My silver boards get courage then,
Try harder now to stand.
But times have changed and years have passed,
No one to hold the torch.....
I wait here patient, looking on
A lifetime on my porch.

Picture by Ruth Scruggs, her family home

# It's Near 'Bout Time

For two thousand years the story's been told,
Of angels surrounding his birth,
Of salvation plan, given to man,
Of Jesus returning to earth.

*Picture by John E. Killett*

For hundreds of years, the sermons were preached,
Men listened while others had mass,
None will have loss that have bowed at the cross,
Thru centuries now that have passed.

152

There's a storm brewing on the horizon,
Seen by all the saved and devout,
For they see the truth, the aged, the youth
And listen for Jesus to shout.

For decades the worst has been brought out in man,
We listen as all the bells chime,
And think we can win by blinking at sin
And one day will run out of time.

Eastern skies are beginning to clear now,
The signs have created no doubt,
I watch yonder sky and ready my eye
As Jesus prepares to step out.

# The Last Brick

Smoke has long since blown away
And lifted to the sky,
Along with smells of grinding cane
And sweet potato pie.
Ferns and weeds have all stretched forth,
The rain is their reward,
While squirrels race along the beams
That hold the silvered board.

*Bell*

And slowly nature hides the home,
The growth without, within,

154

The chimney fights against the vines,
While rust has eaten tin.
So soon it will be all forgot,
So easy to ignore,
And giant oaks will shed their leaves
And shade the home no more.
The stories will be buried 'neath
The ivy, trees, so thick,
And someone in the years to come
Will kneel and find a brick.
And wonder at the strewn boards
And strain their ears to hear,
The voices from so long ago,
That speak when you were here.

# Grassy Fields

A dust devil blows across the ridge,
I watch, then look ahead
To grassy fields that fall away,
Some see grass, I see the dead.

I hear the flies that buzz and feed,
Lay their eggs in eyes and mouth,
I tremble at the view I see,
The price paid highly by the South.

I see the mounds of bloated men,
It's hard to take a breath,
Horses still, their eyes a glaze,
Some see grass, I smell the death.

Cries filter through the smoky haze
That covers field from sight
And as I watch the scene unfold,
Cries grow quiet in the night.

The wildflowers now push above,
But I see only red,
I kneel and touch the holy ground,
Some see vistas, I see dead.

I see men moved without their legs,
Laid quickly on a cot,

There's some, no arms and some no feet,
So many belly shot.

My tears begin to trickle down,
As mounded parts grow high,
Parts of men are now a pile,
While others wait to die.

And you want this to be erased,
Our history all forgot?
You pull down statues, change our names
And cover up this holy spot.

I taste the powder, hear the drum,
I see where men have bled,
I strain to see across the field,
Some see grass, I see the dead.

# Gulf Hammock Church

The cedar, oak gave all the shade,
To buggies, horse and halter,
They rested under shady trees,
Prayers rested on the alter.
The bell was there when I first came,
The windows were not broke,
It needed paint, it needed love,
 protected by the oak.
I often walked among the pews,
One time I swept the floor,
I closed my eyes and wandered back
To what it was before.
I heard the words of mighty God,
Preached from the pulpit there,
I saw the ones excepting Christ,
I heard their earnest prayer.
I saw it as the school house,
Saw trees the children climb,
Saw blackboard, chalk, the old ink well
They used far back in time.
I saw it as the meeting house
That kept Gulf Hammock sound,
But most of all when I walked in
The walls said, "Holy ground."
But now the bell no longer tolls,
Someone has cut it's rope
And as the years plod slowly on

There's not much left in hope.
The pews have long since disappeared,
Trees fell against it's side,
The shards of windows that are left
All say this place has died.
Yet still the creek meanders on,
Like those that came to pray
And as it passes near this spot
It watches the decay.
I still go in from time to time,
Walk careful on the floor
And strain my ears to hear again
The prayers that went before.
The roof is finally caving in,
The weeds have choked the lawn.
I fear the day that soon will come......
Old Florida is gone.

19th Century Gulf Hammock Florida Community School

# Rust, Rot and Razed

As I grow old and look around,
It seems I am amazed
At what we leave to rust and rot
And what we let be razed.
A tired truck out in the field,
The trees have grown 'round,
The bed is shot, the tires flat,
The rust, a reddish brown.
It's mirror cracked, shows silhouette
Of something time forgot,
Just down the path it tries to stand,
It's boards decayed with rot.
And there in town a home place stands,
Land worth more than appraised,
The city father's know what's best
And sign to have it razed.
I close my eyes against the view
At all their power, lust,
My pleas to keep have filled their ears,
But all they see is rust.
A homestead on a country farm
Is pretty, not a blot,
What I see rich in history
The other's see as rot.
While there in town the traffic moves
On land that once was grazed,
A stately home must make more room,

Waits silent to be razed.
Now in a lifetime change must come,
I fear our past is sold
And I, like trucks and silver boards
Am fading, growing old.
I always stop and look around,
Our past I've always praised
And thank the Lord I got to see
The rusty, rotted, razed.

# Secrets

They say that in the murky swamp
The mist is thick until it clears
And leaves will hide the worn path
And secrets live a hundred years.
The whispers of the canopy
Shade dry land and the slough
And time will claim their secrets back,
Not leaving us a clue.
Moss and fern now cover roof
And push against the eaves
And hush the saplings that have grown,
O're what's beneath the leaves.
They say that in the murky swamp,
Time passes still and slow,
Not bush, nor tree, nor coon or bird
Will talk of long ago.
They will not speak of pooling blood
That night, so far from town,
That night their grandson came for them,
The night the ax came down.
But when the winds begin to blow
There under darkened sky,
The swamp will gather all her strength
To muffle dying cry.
For Isham Stewart and his wife,
No longer lay in bed,
Their grandson holds the dripping ax,

And stands right overhead.
Was just a week before the swamp
Saw cops there in the yard,
Their bloated bodies still inside,
With vultures all on guard.
They say that in the murky swamp,
Two headstones, old and worn,
Peek out from years of falling leaves,
Through weeds and through the thorn.
A hundred years, the swamp is still,

The mystery she will hold,
Walls have withered, fallen in,
But still she hasn't told.
Metal roof has rusted through,
No splendor and no pomp
And slowly Stewart's old homestead
Will be part of the swamp.

The plaque reads:

STEWART HOMESTEAD

MR. & MRS.
STEWART

ISHAM (ISOM) and SARAH (SALLIE)
1860 - MAY 9, 1918    1845 - MAY 9, 1918

Axe Murdered together in their home

By Sallie's Grandson Joshua Browning and his friend John Tucker

*Pictures by John E. Killett*

164

## The Shape of Water

The coolness of the muddy creek
Has touched my fevered brow
And fleeting thoughts have taken me
From where I am right now.
In distant corners of my mind,
I feel the thorny hedge,
When Momma picked the berries there,
I played along the edge.
I'd catch the frog and minnows then,
The creek seemed so alive,
I studied prints along the shore
Before I was yet five.
Along a stretch the water pooled,
Us boys would climb a limb;
We learned to smoke, we learned to cuss,
Was here we learned to swim.
And so the water touched my life,
Was every young boy's wish,
I'd steal away from plowing fields,
Trade traces for a fish.
Fast moments I would steal away,
The brothers I would dowse
With buckets filled near to the brim
And carried to the house.
A tub was never meant for boys,
The creek would get us clean,

We lived around the water's edge
When I was just sixteen.
Was here the waters washed my sins,
Right after springtime rise,
When me and Jacob held our breath,
Walked in and both baptized.
Now the creek runs red with blood,
I barely am alive,
Gut shot and lying on the edge,
Now only twenty-five.
And yet the creek still calms my soul,
From memory I hear,
The words to "Crossing Jordon"
Are ringing in my ear.
The water flows around the bend
And swirls 'round my head,
The cannon's fade and shouts grow dim
And leave behind the dead.
I wonder if someone will come,
I'm still and try to pray,
Along the water I have known,
My home a mile away.

# The Rusty Nail

It sits beneath the tangled growth,
Decayed with weathered grime
And clings to ground it covers now,
But years have taken time,
To weaken oaks that once stood proud
And shaded family there,
Each creeping vine now takes it's toll,
Each tree so unaware
That as they fall and near the house,
The crashing of their weight,
Will cover soon this family home
And seal up it's fate.
I make my way or'e fallen limbs,
I've done this all before
And see again another house,
No screens, no floor nor door.
I let it's quiet fill my soul
Before I enter in,
I wipe the blood that trickles down
From brambles biting skin.
I wonder at the rotten boards,
That let the old house stand
And guard the plot it sits upon
Where families farmed the land.
The ghosts have welcomed me inside,
My heart begins to pound,
I feel the sadness and despair

Of those that's gathered 'round.
I hear a lullaby of love
Waft lightly through the wall,
A shadow of a man appears,
Sun burned, unkempt and tall.
And soon the past has beckoned me,
To leave would be to hard,
So followed wispy sounds of love
That led me to the yard.
I saw her then, her back was bent,
Looked frail, sad and weak,
Was but a moment, as I stared,
A tear fell from her cheek.
I watched her wipe the tear away
And dry cheeks on her sleeves,
A tiny stone with chiseled words
Now lay beneath the leaves.
A baby's name, a birth, a death,
Were carved so neatly there,
I felt the sadness in the ghosts
And offered up a prayer.
The silence of the rising mist,
Then pulled them all away,
I knelt and cleared the old stone off
From years of rot, decay.
Then as I left, I touched a board,
Looked sadly at the tin,
I took a nail that partially held
And thanked the ghosts within.
I have a box where treasures stay,
I often touch and grieve
Or'e things that hold old history
And things old houses leave.
The house still peeks between the trees

And ivy covers trail,
Sometimes at night I pray for her
And hold the rusty nail.

*Fort White*

# The River's Edge

I pulled canoe up to the shore,
Laid paddle down inside,
The Withlacoochee water flowed
Past Blue Run's great divide.
I sat beneath the gnarled oak,
Looked east, west and across,
At cypress with their boney limbs,
Draped neatly by the moss.
I saw the red man of the past,
Scoop water to his mouth,
This ole river flowed on north,
While others all flowed south.
I watched as he speared one fish, two
And never made a sound.
I sat so still on river bank,
For ghosts were gathered round.
A gator bellowed from a cove,
An otter splashed in play,
A lazy bass swam close to me,
He circled, moved away.
I focused on the other bank,
A wagon slowed and stopped,
A farmer knelt and took a drink
And studied yonder crop.
For there just past the timberline,
In shadows of the morn,
I barely saw his cracker house

Amid the cotton, corn.
Down thru the years the river flows
And time still marches forth,
The red, the white, the slave, the free...
This river moving north.
The trees have anchored deep within,
The silt of sand and clay
And watched the rise and fall of floods
While years have passed away.
I swish my foot at water's edge,
Watch circles as they grow
And think how little this has changed
From years so long ago.
I watch as does dart thru the trees,
As kites hang in the sky.
I breath in deep as those before
And whisper a good-by.
I paddle back thru all the years,
Was such a privilege,
To see it then, to see it now
Appear at water's edge.

*Withlacoochee River*

## Faith

I've read his letter ten times ten and try to find the signs
Of something I have missed before, between the worn lines.
He wrote to me of dusty roads, left out the raucous terms,
Described the biscuits, quickly fixed, the meal filled with worms.

He once wrote me how bad the heat would sizzle on the ground,
How yankee soldiers picked them off from hedgerows all
around.

How long the marches were between the days of bloody fray,
and often he would write of men that died along the way.
He'd write of respites from the cold, the dreary owl's hoot,
He often wrote of blistered feet from ragged, worn boot.
He once wrote of a horse he rode, a gray from head to tail,
But somewhere in Virginia hills, it died along the trail.
But yet this letter does not seem as long as those before,
I try to read between the lines, his last one of the war.
He said he was at Gettysburg, that fighting's not begun,
And as he always done before, he signed it, "Loving Son."
For fifty years I've read his words and try to find the signs,
To tell me why he's not come home, I read between the lines.
But hands now shake and eyes are dim, yet still I haven't heard,
Each day I straighten letters out and study every word.
Somewhere it must be written here, among the letters stacked,
Each day I try to read and find why he has not come back.

## The Gate Keeper

The rain clouds were just threatening,
When the wind began to gust,
She sadly watched her dying fields
blow away to dust.
She watched the corn in thirsty rows
And wondered at her fate,
She offered up a prayer for rain
And watched the garden gate.
It's been so long since they've left home,
The years have passed away,
But still she watches faithfully
For all her sons in gray.
She once heard Yankees were close by,
She once heard cannons roar,
She once heard soldiers riding up
And banging on her door.
But now her withered hands are stiff,
Her fingers ache with pain,
Her eyes have grown much dimmer
As she stares down dusty lane.
Each browning stalk was dying slow
Refusing to stand straight,
Always as she worked the fields
She watched the garden gate.
She waited for a word to come,
To tell her all was well,
She cringed each time she heard the toll

From distant churchyard bell.
She prayed her boys would come home soon,
That none would be found slain.
She watched the drying field for corn
And prayed that night for rain.
There were no stars or moon to shine,
The hour was quite late,
When from her chair near fireplace
She heard the rusty gate.
So feeble now, she wandered out
For sons that are not there.
She held to fencepost yanks had left
And cried in her despair.
The rain began to pelt the ground,
As thunder shook the land;
Time and hardship takes their toll
And reaches for her hand.
But now a smile has erased
The lines of bitter tears
And God's great hand has pushed aside
The heartache of her years.
Her corn has grown, tasseled high,
Her rows were planted straight,
Her sons have come to guide her thru
The final garden gate.

## In the Candle's Glow

I listened to the crying winds, quite far into the night,
I knew I couldn't pass the chance, would need a little light.
The rain was pelting on the glass, the winds not yet a roar,
The trees were swerving, branches bent, Katrina at the door.
I lit the candle, let it fill the room with light and smell
And watched the flicker of the flame, for stories it would tell.
It took me past the gnarled oak, their branches sweeping low,
I followed down the winding path, thru dust of long ago.
The air was still and heavy there, like caught in someone's
squeeze,
The skies had darkened just a bit, but still there was no breeze.
I saw the wispy outline, from the light the candle shed,
I stared into the wavering light, a gallery right ahead.
It seemed as if there was no one, to welcome me within.
The rain began in mighty drops that wet me to the skin.
I quickly stepped unto the porch, as thunder rumbled low,
I thought I saw a negress maid, as wind began to blow.
I pushed against the unlocked door, a respite from the night,
A parlour on the left of me, a parlour to my right.
I thought I saw a shadow then, a negress near the flame,
By dim and smoky candlelight, she asked me why I came.
I told her of my stormy night, and how I found her there.
She sat and pondered all I said, while rocking in her chair.
"You speck's me to believe in dat, a tale you tellin' me,
I knows there is no step in time, you's here, that's what I see."
And while we talked the wind grew loud, it changed to cold from
warm,

She rocked and wrung her hands again, "Dis be a mighty storm."
And while the shutters swang and clanked and swung from where they hung,
Her toothless smile began to tell, of days when she was young.
"I used to serve the missy, her needs was then my path,
I combs her hair, I met her needs, I even warmed her bath."
Her toothless smile began to fade, the house shook high and low.
"Dis be another hurricane, we had one long ago.
It killed my Missy way back then, the night be dark and grim,
I made it to de second flor, but Missy couldn't swim.
De riber covered parlour flor, it came way past my head,
An when de riber finally lef, my Missy lay here dead."
She asked me if my candle light, revealed that in it's flame,
She told me more of Missy then, Katrina was her name.
Was then my candle flickered out, to soon for me it seemed,
I listened to the gusting wind and then began to dream.
I saw the pooling water grow, I heard the break of bough
And in my dream I couldn't tell, if it were then or now.

# The Staircase

The porch is now decayed with rot,
It's pillars barely stand;
Ivy grows amongst the ruins,
Trees cover most the land.
The mountains whisper of the past
And willows bend to hear,
The wild daffodil still grow,
where once the land was clear.
The bricks have crumbled where one steps
And turned back into dust,
I peeked into the door less jam,
Eyes waiting to adjust.
I walked inside to look around,
Was dark and dank, despair;
Mildewed walls were caving in,
The rooms were drab and bare.
But as my eyes perceived the gloom,
I saw a mystic sight;
A curving staircase, winding up,
All bathed in shafts of light.
I wondered at the marble floor,
The rest were warped with rot.
I marveled at the scene I saw,
The beauty of this spot.
Was then I heard the burley voice,
From bent and whiskered man,
"Missy took care of dis place,"

And thus he then began.
"She used to walk along the path,
Beneath the willow trees
And where she passed magnolia blooms
Would scent the summer breeze..
She used to smile," and on his face
A toothy grin appeared,
I waited for a moment there
Until his thoughts had cleared.
A wrinkled hand went to his brow,
He said his name was John.
He wiped away a bit of dust
And his story then went on.
"She waited here," and pointed to
The fourth plank in the stair,
"It's where he kissed my Missy girl
And touched her golden hair.
Soon walks grew short and hair began
To turn to silver gray
And most her friends and family
All died or moved away.
She waited, first thru days, then years
And yet he never came;
She wasted way to nothing then,
Oh Lord, it was a shame."
He shuffled over to the spot
And cursed the sad affair,
His gnarled finger touched the tread,
Four steps up in the stair.
"I finds her there one stormy night,
Crumpled in a heap,
I thought at first she'd fallen down
Or maybe just asleep.
She's waited here for many years,"

He paused to get his breath;
"The kiss that brushed against her lips
Stayed with her till her death.
I buried her in yonder field
In unused wedding gown
And now you sees the light above,
It's Missy looking down."
I oft have wondered through the years
If house is standing there
And Missy's light is shining down
Upon the winding stair.
It's been a long ten years or so
And now I'm going back,
I wonder what I now will find
As folded clothes are packed.
As I drive the miles away
I wonder if it's gone.
The winding stair, the shaft of light,
The burley man called John.
I stopped to get a room that night
And asked the night clerk there,
If there was something he could tell
About this sad affair.
"No ma'am," he said, "It's all gone
And John has passed away,
The house, you know was fallen down
And rotted with decay."
But still I trudged thru all the weeds,
Pushed briars all aside,
And thought perhaps I'd lost my way,
Just memories to guide.
But there it was, the daffodils
Among the aftermath
Of stormy nights and howling wind,

They grew along the path.
The willows swayed as I walked by,
The briars tried to save
The rusty iron railing
That held in all the graves.
I knelt and pushed aside the years
Of dirt, of weeds and leaf,
I shuttered at the stones I found
And read in disbelief.
Missy's stone was almost smooth,
Though marble color bright,
Was when the clouds began to form
I saw the shaft of light.
It shone upon a cherub there,
Weathered, gray and drab,
The nettles stopped before they touched
The tiny little slab.
I wondered at the stories here
And how it had  begun,
My fingers outlined all the words,
"Here lies my only son."
Just feet away I saw the mound
With just a cross upon,
I pulled away the trailing vines
And saw the name of John.
I sat awhile and said some prayers
Upon this saddened land
And knew I'd never know the truth
Or even understand.
As I stopped to turn around
To whisper a good-by,
A shaft of light showed all that's left,
A staircase, four steps high.

It's been a long ten years or so
And now I'm going back,
I wonder what I now will find
As folded clothes are packed.
As I drive the miles away
I wonder if it's gone.
The winding stair, the shaft of light,
The burley man called John.
I stopped to get a room that night
And asked the night clerk there,
If there was something he could tell
About this sad affair.
"No ma'am," he said, "It's all gone
And John has passed away,
The house, you know was fallen down
And rotted with decay."
But still I trudged thru all the weeds,
Pushed briars all aside,
And thought perhaps I'd lost my way,
Just memories to guide.
But there it was, the daffodils
Among the aftermath
Of stormy nights and howling wind,
They grew along the path.
The willows swayed as I walked by,
The briars tried to save
The rusty iron railing
That held in all the graves.
I knelt and pushed aside the years
Of dirt, of weeds and leaf,
I shuttered at the stones I found
And read in disbelief.

Missy's stone was almost smooth,
Though marble color bright,
Was when the clouds began to form
I saw the shaft of light.
It shone upon a cherub there,
Weathered, gray and drab,
The nettles stopped before they touched
The tiny little slab.

I wondered at the stories here
And how it had  begun,
My fingers outlined all the words,
"Here lies my only son."
Just feet away I saw the mound
With just a cross upon,

I pulled away the trailing vines
And saw the name of John.
I sat awhile and said some prayers
Upon this saddened land
And knew I'd never know the truth
Or even understand.
As I stopped to turn around
To whisper a good-by,
A shaft of light showed all that's left,
A staircase, four steps high.

## Holding On

The brick is holding, best it can,
Yet loses every day,
Weathered boards try to regain
What termites eat away.
Trees have grown up thru the floor
And push at every crack,
While spiders, wasps, bugs and mold
All plan their next attack.
I peer into the door less dark,
Not much more than a shed,
And push away the cobwebs
That I feel 'round my head.
I hear the old place sigh in grief,
Soon to be no more,
The cracks of time have let sun in,
In shafts across the floor.
I guess some miss the solitude
I see in what it gives,
There in the darkness of it's past,
A quiet beauty lives.
It seems it's just like growing old,
My mirror says it's so.
Each year I look, I'm not the same
As I was long ago.
So I look past the broken boards,
Thru windows without pane,
I close my eyes, push back the years

And see it young again.
Before the years have left their mark
On doors, on floors, on shelf,
I look past to the younger times,
With houses and myself!
For I know well you can not stop
The years that are your prime,
For darkened doors and mirrored truth
Are moments caught in time.

*Picture by Charlotte Kolbe*

## Testament to Time

The morning dawned bright and fair,
Few clouds were in the sky,
Crops had grown great that year,
The corn was five feet high.
My mistress and my master
Had left to go to town,
That morning when the sky was blue,
Before the rains came down.
At first I heard the rumbling
Way past the planted pine,
Out there the sky had darkened,
But here was still sunshine.
The air had grown hotter,
Past morning', thru the day
And now the dark horizon
Was not so far away.
The breeze had turned to blowing
And the clouds seemed to descend,
The oaks were swooshing in the wind
And corn began to bend.
Wind gusted 'round my corners,
Soon rain came down in squalls,
Pushed against my window panes
And pelted on my walls.
The noise it brought was deafening,
I needed no more proof,
The storm was coming 'cross the field

And aiming at my roof.
I felt my timber cracking,
 I heard my shutters sway,
My roof flew into darkness,
 I felt my walls give way.
So soon it past and left a path
Of summer storm and theft,
Now parts of what I used to be
Is all destruction left.
I watch the years plod slowly on,
Protecting two old chairs,
Full knowing that I'm well past help
And well past all repairs.
My timbers creak and partly fall,
No one will occupy,
But broken windows fight to hold
The sight of who comes by.
This morning dawned so bright and fair,
I'm shaded by the trees,
Forgotten shack out in the field,
Just home to mice and bees.
My old planks pull at nails put in
From years of long ago
And in the distance I can hear
A rumbling start to grow.
Clouds are forming past the pines.
I try to judge the length
Of time it takes for rain and wind
To push against my strength.
Perhaps this day will pass as calm
And skies will remain clear
And let me be a testament
For just another year.

*Picture by Andrea Sadock*

## The Bench

He sat there quiet on the bench,
His head held by a hand,
While eyes stared blankly straight ahead,
He tried to understand.
He stared at cold and chiseled stone
And wondered why he came,
He knew each plot laid out in rows,
Each stone that had no name.
His hands began to shake a bit,
He lifted up his head
And in the quiet of this place,
He walked among the dead.
So many men he did not know,
Yet fought here side by side,
So many men he tried to help
And watched them as they died.
He held the water to their mouth
And tried hard not to think
Of gaping hole and gurgled breath
As they tried hard to drink.
And often when men breathed their last,
Was hard for him to stand
The sight of shredded, dying men
Now holding to his hand.
He stood and leaned against the bench,
His right leg bent and lame,
He strained his eyes so he could see

The stones without a name.
He hobbled through the many rows
And touched the cold, gray stone,
Remembered how he gathered men,
Their parts, the body, bone.
Once more the cannons roared and smoked,
He saw so many fall,
He saw the gut shot blown away,
He watched the others crawl.
The horses reared and some were spooked,
Some fell where they were shot;
Now men that he had tried to help
Were buried 'neath this spot.
He limped back to the iron bench
And tried to justify
All the stones without a name,
He sighed and closed his eyes.
There in the softness of the eve,
When light is dusty, low,
He thought of men without a name,
All someone, no one knows.
And now I walk between the rows,
Think how this place has grown.
There is no silence in this spot,
I touch the chiseled stone.
I feel the letters carved upon
The tombstones of my past
And soon I see the battle rage,
I hear the cannon's blast.
I hear the balls whiz through the trees,
Gunpowder makes me choke,
I fight to find a safe way out
Through mangled men and smoke.
I make it to the old, worn bench,

I barely now can stand.
Though I'm alone amidst the tombs,
I feel a gentle hand.
I can barely see the shadow,
An old man, bent and maim,
We sit together looking out
At stones that have no name.

*Picture by John E. Killett*

## Acknowledgements

I would like to thank each contributor that allowed me to use their pictures. They have led me to places I might never have seen and I deeply appreciate the paths they have led me down.

Made in the USA
Columbia, SC
22 July 2019